FAITH'S LAST HURRAH!

Poems
Rhymes
and
Limericks

Bruce David Prewer

Ideas into Books: Westview®
Kingston Springs, TN USA

Ideas into Books: WESTVIEW®
P.O. Box 605
Kingston Springs, TN 37082
www.publishedbywestview.com

ISBN 978-1-62880-135-4

First edition, January 2018

FOREWORD

This is most likely the last volume that will be published under my name: A collection of over 200 poems, rhymes, and limericks—about 80% of which have not hitherto been published—constitutes my final *Hurrah!*

My health makes the title inevitable. Apart from a debilitating blood disorder and some recent challenging episodes with cancer, for some years I have been entrusted with a Parkinson's Plus Disease–Progressive Supranuclear Palsy. Its inexorable attack on my mental "motor skills" has not only disabled handwriting, balance, mobility, speech, eating, and sleeping, but I can no longer use my keyboard PC, except by (literally) the tedious employment of a sole index finger.

All of my previous publications have been an attempt at *Hurrah!*: A cheering for the extraordinary gospel of Messiah Jesus with "*grace heaped upon grace*" at work in our ordinary lives. I have sought to celebrate these glimpses of the abundant mercies of God glistening in every facet of secular daily-ness. This collection of poems falls into that same genre.

The progression of disease makes this final *Hurrah!* even more emphatic. I now know, existentially, the God of Jesus is indeed present with me in every moment of decline and I want to celebrate that Presence with all my residual being! I have another favourite Bible text:

"The light shines in the darkness and the darkness cannot smother it."

With this text I present the following poems, rhymes, and limericks as one elderly pastor's testament to the grace-gift of a personal faith which transcends a plethora of doubts.

Bruce David Prewer

TABLE OF CONTENTS

MESSIAH JESUS: NOW AND THEN 37

LOVING THE UNSEARCHABLE GOD

LOVE

1 John 4:7-12

Here is the key
which will unlock
the obscure Cause
truly unsearchable
since the 'big bang'
gifted time and space.

Here is the clue
which will reveal
the rich source
beneath faith and hope
and the true light
of every race.

Here is the crux
which will unveil
the driving force
of genes, stem cells,
and the wonder
in each child's face.

Here is the end
to which we rise
beyond remorse
and the Alpha Joy
which is attained
solely by grace.

PERSPECTIVE

The Awesome Spirit
knitted my frayed faith
and in one moment
set me on a high
yet very lowly place.

I saw the whole majesty
of the human story
unfolding before me
from the first nomads
to Mother Theresa's smile.

Abraham and Sarah passed by
Nefertiti flowered and faded
Homer recited his verse
Rome marched triumphant
and Light exploded in Bethlehem.

John penned his Gospel
Francis and Clare fed the poor
Leonardo painted Mona Lisa
Mozart eavesdropped on heaven
Einstein deciphered a mystery.

In one moment of Light
the amazing human story
of one small planet's dust
resplendent, blazing brilliantly:
I beheld our glory!

Yet all was contained in just one
drop of overnight dew
on one needle of one she-oak
disclosed briefly in the glow
of the rising sun.

SEASIDE BENEDICTION

The evening gannets bank and dive
with grace supreme
the waves turn over sand and shells
as in a dream.

From mangroves near an estuary
a curlew cries
regrets and fears from long past years
within me rise.

A mild wind fans my greying hair
like something blest
the Word within a word says, "Come
to me and rest."

TO THE ONE I ADORE

You are the questions in my creed
and the creed within my doubt.
You are the joy that throbs like pain
and the grief I can't do without.

You are the light within my darkness
and the night within my day.
You are the loss in my success
and the gain in my dismay.

You are the stillness in my prayers
and the prayer within my deeds.
You are the weakness in my strength
and the power within my needs.

You are the illness in my best health
and my health within disease.
You are the hunger in my content
and the content within my pleas.

You are the void to which I cling
and the fullness I can't possess.
You are the tears in my delight
and the rapture I can't express.

You are the stress that brings me peace
and the peace I crave the more.
You are the meek who makes me proud
and the Friend that I adore.

LOVING YOU

You, whom some call
God, Yahweh, Allah, Krishna
or the great Uncaused Cause,
I am loving you
because you first chose
to be loving us all:

In the thirst that impels us
the enigma that stalls us
the stream that bathes us
the optimism that lifts us
the lamp that guides us
the bread that feeds us;

You are the Awesome End
which purposed that lovely Jew
Messiah Jesus
to the Cross and beyond:
In him we come face to face
with our one, Absolute Friend:

In his joy that blind-sides us
his calm that stills us
his arms that hold us
his mercy that saturates us
his warmth that enfolds us
and his death that frees us.

You, whom many call
God, Yahweh, Allah, Krishna
or the great Uncaused Cause,
I am loving you
because you first chose
to be loving us all.

LEAP OF FAITH

I plunge
into the immense ocean
of the Ineffable Mystery
so large
so wide
yet so deep
that I should not be able
to get any footing;

Yet I find it so
welcoming, warm
safe and secure
cathartic
and healing
that I know
at last—at long, long last,

I am coming home!

ALWAYS THERE IS GRACE

Before the first day there was Grace
far preceding time and space,
dreaming hopes of magnitude
ready with all plenitude.

On this planet there is Grace
tireless working in each place,
mercy that is so profound
that we walk on sacred ground.

In life's travail there is Grace
underwriting every race,
caring when one soul gets lost
saving at prodigious cost.

In the humblest Outback stable
at the highest Holy Table:
at our dying there'll be Grace
wearing still a mortal face;

At the Rapture there'll be Grace
superseding time and space;
welcoming the last and least
to the simplest, Joy-full Feast.

POOR SUBSTITUTES

Much of folk religion
and pious phrases
    are cramped cages
in which we attempt
to hijack the Word
    and privatise God.

We only hear the Word
when we scrap the cages
    and stand impotent.
Even then, if we try
to possess the Word
    it becomes a chimera.

All god-words can be idols;
creeds are poor icons
    briefly aiding us
but are poor substitutes
for the raw, living Word;
    All that matters is YOU!

THANKS FOR THINGS FINITE

That our hands, feet, and muscles,
blood cells, brain cells,
our DNA and genetic codes
are finite:
Blessed be God!
Blessed be God forever!

That our money and possessions
status, fame, or titles
houses, mansions, and palaces
are finite:
Blessed be God!
Blessed be God forever!

That skyscrapers and monuments
sacred sites and cathedrals
maths, science, and technology
are finite:
Blessed be God!
Blessed be God forever!

That the world and its creatures
sun, moon, and milky way
the awesome span of time and space
are finite:
Blessed be God!
Blessed be God forever!

That Jesus and his parables
the Commonwealth of God
and faith, hope, and love
are Infinite:
Blessed be God!
Blessed be God forever!

That by the grace that grants faith
by the cross and empty tomb
by the tireless thrust of the Spirit
we share Infinity:
Blessed be God!
Blessed be God forever!

GOD IS LOVE

Unlikely as life's gestation
unexpected as incarnation:
God is love.

Simple as salt and yeast
humble as the last and least:
God is love.

Grace-full as the lame walking
joy-full as the dumb talking:
God is love.

Fearsome as crucifixion
awesome as resurrection:
God is love.

Limerick:
TRINITY

There was a saint up in Bright
who loved God with all her might
when asked to explain
and make Trinity plain
she said: "I get lost in its light."

FAITH THAT DOUBTS

Give praise to God for faith that doubts
the world that brays around us;
thank God for that small mustard seed
that on the Wind has found us.

By faith we doubt the 'progress' myth
and the latest science fashion;
we do not trust technology
that spawns without compassion.

By faith we doubt Canberra's creeds
with its 'level playing field;'
we doubt that greed delivers good
making the poor well-heeled.

By faith we doubt that Einstein
was more advanced than Dorcus;
or that breaking genetic codes
make us wiser than Jesus.

The worldly wise don't have such doubts
it's not a gift they vie for;
for such a faith let loose on earth
is something God would die for!

THERE IS THIS LIGHT

Elusive but certain, there is this Light
clearer than all other gleaming
that darts around the edges of my sight
by day and even when I'm dreaming.

It inhabits my peripheral vision
like an old friend, the shyest guest
so elusive, though clearer than the sun
there is this Light which does not rest.

'Stay still and let me study you," I sigh
but it flits around the edges of each day
coyly, yet like a gentle mote on the eye
this Light will never go away.

There is this Light, that I would like to tame,
when sometimes it takes central place
but stays just for a brief fleck of time
before it flits back to its furtive space.

Yet in it's wondrous brevity are all
colours of God's rainbow and much more
more lovely than a guardian angel's soul
there is this Light, which I adore.

TO THE MYSTERY

Deep Mystery:
we paddle freely in your warm shallows
and on sunny days surf the waves near our shore
but forever your depths are unfathomable;
Deep Mystery!

High Mystery:
we hike around the fringes of your foothills
and on brave days climb almost to your ankles
but forever your heights are unattainable;
High Mystery!

Wide Mystery:
we measure time-space within your cosmic reaches
and on clear nights calculate the span to Andromeda
but forever your breadth is immeasurable;
Wide Mystery!

Christ Mystery:
you come our way in humble truth and grace
wearing our smell and sharing our common daily-ness
and forever you are available and vulnerable.
Christ Mystery!

BURIED TREASURE

Matthew 3:14

This world is not a futile field
though doubts abound
our days are meant for light and love
so rarely found
mere infants know that every place
is holy Ground.

Men worry much and toil too hard
for tawdry fame
in business or in pop careers
they make their name
yet meek and poor know fame can't buy
the sacred Flame.

The gifts of God like sun and rain
are always free
and faith and love are not rewards
for industry
the pure of heart look on that Face
eyes cannot see.

The clowns of God do not resign
to fear and doom
they make us chuckle at ourselves
dispelling gloom
for in their mirth they've buried death
in Jesus' tomb.

BRIEF ENCOUNTERS

By the edge of my eye
a fleeting glimpse
of Light
the worldly can't see
nor I convince;
exceeding dawn and dusk
and moonlit plains
more lovely than rainbows
in springtime rains.

At the infra-range of ears
a song sublime
of Music
that's been there
before all time;
beyond Bach and Mozart
at their choicest best
a harmony in which
sore souls find rest.

Near the rhythm of my heart
a larger beat
the Pulse
of the Unseen
we long to greet;
It's surely from that Grace
I long have known
such rugged love belongs
to Christ alone.

WHERE IS GOD?

Mark 6:14-19

Where is God
   when prophet John
   is beheaded
   at the request
   of a belly dancer?

Where is God
   when devout families
   are slaughtered
   while at prayer
   in village churches?

Where is God
   when raging Moslem
   and vengeful Jew
   murder each other
   in the name of faith?

Where is God
   when Mary's Child
   gets nailed to a cross
   and dies forsaken
   in the name of God?

Is it that same
   cross Lord, which not only
   absolutes our questions
   but gives us a reply
   signed with Divine blood?

WITH THE MEEK AND POOR

God stands in the open door
comes with our every breath
lives with the meek and poor
travails in birth and death.

God dances among the meek
laughs in an infant's mirth
finds those who truly seek
gives faith eternal worth.

God aches with the hungry child
redeems the past we leave
groans with a world gone wild
and smiles in hopes we weave.

God attends a struggling church
sings with each melody
inspires the preacher's search
breaks bread in community.

THE VOICE

John 1 & Genesis 1

Yours is the Voice that spoke at the beginning
and a universe that never was, came to be.

Yours is the Voice that was at the beginning
there with the Unbegan, that Holy Other
and all the Unbegan ever was or will be
so too is my Voice with you, for ever.

Yours is the Voice that bespoke all things
galaxies, sun, moon, earth, and seas;
all that lives, breathes by this Voice:
bumble bee, bison, dolphin, and kookaburra.

Yours is the Voice that speaks life and light
into homo sapiens, woman, man, child:
yours the Unbegan that speaks in the darkness
and the darkness can never quench it!

Yours is the Voice who became incarnate
overflowing with the glory of grace and truth
while the morning stars sing together
and all the heavenly host shout for joy!

COME AWAY WITH ME

Mark 6:30-32

Come away with me
to a lonely place
   where I may kneel
   and vent my pain
   to the wilderness.

Come away with me
to a lonely place
   where I may shout
   my lurking doubts
   at the wilderness.

Come away with me
to a lonely place
   where I may wrestle
   the God who calls
   from the wilderness.

Come away with me
to a lonely place
   where I may leave
   my gnawing fears
   with the wilderness.

Come away with me
to a lonely place
   where I may claim
   God's peace that waits
   in the wilderness.

INSPIRED BY PSALM 139

God, you search my ways and plumb
the darkest deeps of my brain
you know me through and through.
You see when I fall and when I stand tall
you are with me in achievement
or in failure and in pain.

If I am swept up on the wings of time
and find myself back at the "Big Bang"
I will find your love there;
If I soar into the future to the final implosion
of time and space
you will still be there for me.

Though I'm disabled by stroke or neuro disease,
and can no longer speak or write
you will still commune with me.
Should dementia overwhelm my mind
and utterly bewilder
your arms will enfold and cherish me.

Should a total darkness engulf me
and I weep hot tears like a lost child
night will become bright as day.
Should a giant meteor strike the earth
leaving me among the remnant left alive
you will never leave me forsaken.

Holy Friend, from everlasting to everlasting
you are the God of the least and lost
nothing will ever change that.
I am your adopted child
made a joint-heir with Jesus
your only true, ever-redeeming Son.

Continue to search me and know my thoughts
see all error and eradicate evil within me;
save me from temptation
and deliver me from evil;
gather me into the glory
of your light perpetual.

PLANTING SYCAMORES

Luke 17:5-6

I said to the man from Galilee:
"How many sycamores grow in the sea?"
 He answered with a grin on his face:
"As many as you who live by grace."

ABANDONED POEMS

You're far yet close
so vast, so small?
You leave my words and phrases
no where to go at all.

Priceless yet free
dead end yet door?
You scatter all my matchstick words
upon the library floor.

The King who's pawn
Judge in the dock?
You upend thoughts and hint at codes
mere brains cannot unlock.

You're pen, and Word
the known Unknown?
Your holy ways are not my ways
yet I never write alone.

You're thirst yet peace
sore loss though gain?
You watch me flush unfinished
many poems down the drain.

TO THE UNTAMABLE GOD

Holy One, source and sustenance
breath of mercy, fire of faith,
we say the name "God"
as we love and worship you;

Yet these are only the fringes
of your majestic ways
so small is the whisper
that we have heard from you.

The more we raise our voices
or pour concrete creeds
the more it is embarrassingly obvious
how little we really know of you;

And even how much less
we have understood from you.
Yet by grace we eagerly celebrate
the little that has grasped us:

In Christ we know you are Love
present in all times and all places;
and you are without fail, always
here for each one of us.

Blessed are all who glimpse you
thrice-blessed those who trust you!
Holy, Holy, most Holy Friend,
all things are full of glory!

ARRIVING LATE

Acts 3

We arrived late at Pentecost
after the fun was over
Peter's sermon finished
the baptisms completed
and the minutes written.

What was there left?
Let this be recorded
for any who, as they read
employ their soul
as much as their eyes:

We found a communal Gift
priceless yet free
in that heartwood where
the Carpenter had carved
a vacant space.

This Gift that we found
filling that Christ-cavity
(at the end of the day
when the cynics had gone
home to their boredom)

Was the very Soul of Love;
not the old stuff, hedged
with conditions and exemptions
but the new Agape, eager
to embrace the world!

ALL THINGS TO ME

You have a prodigal's welcome for me–
Your house of love, my homeless space,
my coming home, your warm embrace.

You make the world new for me–
Your party time, my cleansing bath,
my new robes, your joyful laugh.

You choose what is best for me–
Your call to serve, my work and toil,
my evening prayers, your midnight oil.

You put no new tax on me–
Your easy yoke, my burden light,
my gratis strength, your star by night.

You give Your own gospel to me–
Your precious pearl, my mustard seed,
my new vision, your new age creed.

You give what will nourish me–
Your Spirit truth, my humble shrine,
my hungry soul, your Bread and Wine.

Your turn defeat into conquest for me–
Your wounded hands, my dispelled doubts,
Your Easter greeting, my Easter shouts.

ELUSIVE SPIRIT

You, elusive Spirit-Truth;
we cannot define you, for you
defy our analytical minds
and smile at silly assumptions.

Yet we know you dearly
like we know beauty and love;
the warm womb of birth and rebirth
the nurturer of faith and hope–

> *as night-fire warding off soul-frost*
> *the sea breeze checking hot anger*
> *the dawn air filling our sleepy lungs*
> *the peace that bottoms out beneath sorrows.*

We do know you nearly:
like almost completed jig-saw fragments
the zest that drives playful puppies
the fire in the gut of prophets–

> *as energy that sends eagles soaring*
> *the geometry behind creative chaos*
> *the thrust of self-transcendence*
> *and light that precedes the Milky Way.*

Yet we know you most clearly
in the joys and pain of Joseph's son;
the source of his Mother's conceiving
the Light from his believing–

the good humour of his teaching
the dynamic of his healing
the blasphemy of his dying
the confounding of his rising.

You, elusive Spirit Truth;
Friend of street kids and the meek
coming and going as you will
Companion to the world's end–

we cannot name you nor tame you
yet with hearts that burn within us
we can love and adore you
the very Kiss of limitless Life!

PRAYING WITH PAINT

An artist is a strange child
who prays with paint
though seldom are they called
'a blessed saint;'
with paint and brush they hint
of untamed Joy
a vision that art critic's spleen
cannot destroy.

A potter is a strange child
who prays with clay
though fingers cannot ever shape
the perfection they pray;
yet they take mud undaunted
believing still
that one day it might yield
to hand and will.

A poet is a strange child
who prays with pen
and though Light eludes words
they'll try again;
they will not bluster or to
trite words succumb
they seem to know the best
is yet to come.

A 'muso" is a strange child
who prays with sound
beneath this world's discord
hears themes profound;
some nights they're woken by
such perfect pitch
as leaves them tingling with
a divine itch.

A preacher is a strange child
who prays with tongue
and wrestles with a Word
forever young;
a hapless cause though this
may seem to be
he is among the first
to be blessed with the
Word's synergy.

POURED OUT

Acts 3:1-18

Spirit, the very Soul of God
that Holy Otherness
with boundless grace
is now poured out
on the human race.

Not allocated sparingly
as from an eye-dropper;
not like tonic in a medicine glass
measured carefully;
not even so generous
as a farmhouse mug of tea;

Poured prodigally:
tumbling and splashing
quenching the thirsty
sparklingly new each day;
refreshing the weary
bountiful as the Milky Way;

Cascading on all people
torrential and flooding:
the very Soul of God
lavishly, immeasurably poured;
drenching each earthling
leaving some ineffably over-awed!

ALL'S WELL

God's in his heaven
all's well with the world.

Robert Browning

God's with the angels
on a heavenly throne;
God's lives in Kings Cross
we're never alone.

God's in his heaven
boat-people have worth;
God is forsaken
his blood seeds the earth.

God's off the planet
space men can't find him;
God is in our heads
yet minds can't bind him.

If God's not in heaven
then earth has no glory;
if God's not on earth
heaven's a vain story.

SAVING GRACE

One day it's an abrasive thing
which storms at me like Simpson sand;
the next day it's the gentlest thing
like a bush orchid in my hand.

I try to pot it for my pleasure
but overnight it grows immense
like a bean stalk without measure
leaving me with no defence.

In the hard times I really wonder
whether it exists at all;
then it storms at me like thunder
and soaks me where I fall.

Grace is an eagle on the wing
soaring to the world's end.
Grace is Gift; a prodigal thing
from the Crucified Friend.

CHILDREN OF THE STARS

Blessed wherever children of the stars
have heard a Whisper
of eternal loving ways
and have responded
giving themselves
utterly
to that still, small Voice, eagerly.

Twice blessed whatever fallen worlds
where by what other name
or in a bizarre shape
Emmanuel has come among them
infra-flooding each and all
utterly
with redemptive creativity.

Thrice blessed chosen planets
that spin their way by remote suns
not left perpetually forsaken
but ever with that nesting Spirit
and faithful, brooding mercy
utterly
making all things pulse with destiny.

MESSIAH JESUS:
NOW AND THEN

UNLIKELY PRINCE

Strangely conceived, born in a shed,
odour of donkeys, straw for your cot,
fleeing by night, price on your head,
a refugee, sharing our lot:
unlikely prince, our humble Lord!

Filling each day, trusting weak blokes,
homeless preacher, fishermen's friend,
sowing small seeds, telling good jokes,
praying alone, at the day's end:
unlikely prince, our humble Lord!

Stretching the mind, opening the ears,
telling the truth, offending old schools,
spurning cheap fame, conquering fears,
led by Spirit, breaking the rules:
unlikely prince, our humble Lord!

Humbling the proud, lifting the meek,
praising the poor, pitying the rich,
fasting alone, strengthening the weak,
lifting the blind out of the ditch:
unlikely prince, our humble Lord!

Hope of sinners, loved by the crowd,
healing lepers, seeking the lost,
prizing the meek, humbling the proud,
taking love's risks, paying the cost:
unlikely prince, our humble Lord!

Fool on a donkey, without back-up,
cleansing the shrine, sealing your fate,
breaking the bread, sharing the cup,
betrayed at night, 'shopped' by a mate:
unlikely prince, our humble Lord.

Tried by a rogue, mocked by a king,
hauling your cross, up to Skull Hill,
lifted up high, forsaken thing,
scorned and despised, forgiving still:
unlikely prince, our humble Lord.

Tended by women, resting in hell,
in a cold tomb, through blackest night
delivering souls, from where they fell,
greeting the dawn, with Easter light:
unlikely prince, our humble Lord!

Always among us, sheep and the goats,
prisoner in chains, sick and the poor,
dearest soul-mate, most blessed Host,
our dearest joy, for ever more:
unlikely prince, our humble Lord!

YOU CONFOUND ME

Messiah Jesus
the 'Joy of loving hearts'
yet lover of enemies:
you utterly confound me.

I comprehend you less
than I thought I knew
seventy years ago
when my faith was young.

No surprise in that;
you've been confounding
human minds
for two millennia:

Son of God?
Son of man?
Eternal Word incarnate
handled by earthings?

Effulgence of God's glory
begotten not made?
Light of True Light
yet carpenter's boy?

Seated at God's right hand
the crucified failure?
Christus Victor
brother yet Lord?

Yes, I'm confounded;
comprehensively lost
as any follower
of You should be!

THE SILENCE

God is the Silence
that swallows up
all our clever words
leaving us stark
gasping for more.

Then while we stand
lost for words
God takes one Sure-Word
and sets it down
upon our shore.

At early dawn
this Word walks our way
wearing deep wounds
without complaint
and we adore.

WHY THIS JESUS?

Sure, there were seers before him
    as there are stars to guide seafarers
and there were saints after him
    as there is lamplight for pilgrims.

But this one disruptive Person
    why does he enthral me?
and why do I want to write 'person'
    with a capital P?

It is not just that he is all
    that humans were meant to be;
rather something larger than life
    a fecund kind of Singularity

Informs his every word and deed
    and makes him more exemplarily
than any seers that ever were
    or saints that are to be.

Sure, there were lights before him
    as starlight precedes the dawn
and there are lights after him
    as the moon reflects the sun.

HE GOES ON AHEAD OF YOU

Matthew 28:7   *"There you shall find him."*

He meets me by the calm Coorong
as pelicans sail by.
I sense him in the Southern Cross
setting over Swan Bay.

He seeks my aid at Alice Springs
with those of battered creed.
I find him busking on the streets,
ignored by the hard crowd.

He waves to me at the MCG
as if he's my best mate.
I watch him greet those bikies
I do not wish to meet.

He joins me down by Bondi Beach
eating a chicko roll.
I meet him in my darkest night
the Realest of things real.

He looks at me in the brown eyes
of a tired traffic cop.
I spot him in the roaring crowd
that cheers the Melbourne Cup.

He bumps me in the Christmas rush
in Brisbane's crowded Mall.
I glimpse him with the Blue Nurses
who go the second mile.

He prays alone up on Kings Park
with Perth's street lights below.
I hear him speak a word of hope
which nothing can belie.

He meets me for a lunch-hour meal
of Launceston where I grew up.
In Adelaide he dines with me
as we share his bread and cup

He sings a song in Kakadu
inside a frescoed cave.
I glimpse him in an old photo
taken at Anzac Cove.

He leaves his tracks of blood around
in many a situation.
We serve him in the rugged task
of reconciliation.

FOR BRUISED REEDS

Mark 1:32-34

Busy Nurse
of faint faith
and fractured creeds;

Healer
of ragged hopes
and secret needs;

Physician
of limping love
and tattered deeds;

Before sunset
lay your hale hands
on all bruised reeds.

TEENAGE PREGNANCY

A teenage pregnancy;
    I saw her moving behind the lattice
    with eyes downcast
    and thought, wrongly, it was
out of shame.

The young body swelling;
    going quietly about her work
    with mind elsewhere
    maybe searching for
the right name?

Veiled and unobtrusive;
    she left to visit her cousin
    Elizabeth, who knew well
    how gossips snigger
and defame.

Weeks later Mary came home
    awkwardly, big with child
    veil now drawn back;
    and I saw her eyes
bold as flame!

IT IS TIME

Mark 1:1-8.

After the pioneers of faith and hope
after the lawgivers and poets
the seers and prophets
and those who fast
in desert places,

Comes a Person who is so grace-full
and so gloriously unpredictable
that predecessors are not fit
to stoop and loose
his sandal laces.

Prepare now a path for his coming
level a smooth track for his feet
for he will bathe with the Spirit
and heaven will smile
on mortal faces.

END AND BEGINNING

At the end of a long journey
for a chosen people
seeking destiny;

At the end of an enforced trek
to a highland Judean town
with no room for the poor;

At the end of a hard travail
for a teenage woman
sheltering in a shed:

Came the unspeakable Gift
an awesome new beginning:
the great folly of God:

A Newborn crying in the night
who frightened jewelled kings
and shook the gates of hell!

VULNERABLE BABY

Such a vulnerable little thing;
wrinkled and daubed with vernix
who coughed and gave a cry;
   the midwife feeling blest
   handed him to the young mother
   who nestled him on her breast.

Such a vulnerable little thing;
bare as a new-hatched galah
blinking at stable lamps;
   the father looked proudly on
   not at all taken aback
   by the frailty of his son.

Such a vulnerable little thing;
Love framed in flesh and blood
the God who's born to die;
   the cattle munched their straw
   and shepherds came to see
   as none ever had before.

BORN WHERE?

They say he was born in Bethlehem
a town in Judean hills;
I think he is born in Sunbury
a town with very few frills.

Some say there were heavenly angels
that sang the night he was born;
I've heard some angelic singing
from children last Sunday morn.

Some say he was born in a cow shed
no room for him with a view;
I know that he found a warm place
in the heart of a plumber I knew.

Some say he arrived with the taxes
that Caesar placed on their land;
I know he comes with free graces
that most don't understand.

Some say his birth was miracle
one-off in the distant past;
I reckon it's still taking place
among the least and the last.

Some claim he will come with power
to finish what love could not do;
I say he comes now in the stranger
waiting in the refugee queue!

THE MAGI

They are still arriving;
some come to kneel
others to stare
drawn by his star.

They gather from the East
South, North, and West;
seeking a light
to redeem night.

They come in their weakness
or in their strength;
seeking a Word
not before heard.

They offer their best gifts
baring their souls;
gold with their prayers
myrrh with their tears.

They leave with hopes newborn
and some heightened fears;
yet in obscurity or fame
never to be the same.

SIMEON

Luke 2:25-31

The old and frail
  will hang on by a thread
  for some special event;
maybe a family wedding
reunion of old army mates
a new grandchild's advent.

Simeon was old
  but not ready to die
  'til his hope found relief;
waiting for Truth revealed
full of such faith and love
that beggared old belief.

At last it came
  into his very arms,
  his heart beating joy-wild;
with a sigh of deep release
he handed back the Child
ready to die now, at peace.

THE WONDER WORD

The Word came among us
completely for us
without meteor or thunder;
born as one of us
the Word incarnate;
yet many will not recognise
this Wonder.

Shepherds knew it;
unwashed and irreligious,
unchurched and illiterate,
at home under open skies.

From that beginning
before the beginning,
the Wonder was there.
Totally beyond us
yet forever with us
embodied here:
the Word of Life.

Those angels came
the messengers from God
with an unlikely announcement
that rationalism decries.

Grace and truth
the elemental Glory
of Wonder on earth;
Light of the True Light
coming to its own
in the common travail
of human birth.

Word In a stable
the smell of dung, an infant's cries
the young mother and newborn son:
a tale only a god could devise.

Limerick:
JESUS

Luke 18:9-14

He was an extraordinary Jew
the soul of grace through and through
tax gatherers and sinners
he made outright winners
while the righteous played cock-a doodle-doo!

EPIPHANY: THREE SWAGMEN

They found him at last
    among the meek and poor.
The three swagmen entered
    through the slab barn door
bearing their precious gifts
    and ready to adore.

They had travelled a long way
    under the southern skies;
plodding through the nights
    following their guiding stars
dozing during hot days
    in the shade of Coolabahs.

Disdained by the town folk
    and evaded by the good;
moved on by the police
    who served a rigid god;
at night the Southern Cross
    their only hope and guide.

Their questions were derided
    their hunger was ignored;
pub keepers threw them out
    and churches were too proud;
the wealthy gave them stones
    the poor shared their bread.

Each found their soul's desire
    on this December dawn;
they washed in a small creek
    and slicked their hair down;
they strode up to the barn
    while corellas made a din.

One gave his precious watch
    handed down from pioneers.
One presented a rough opal
    treasured for many years.
One offered bush Boronia
    wet with fresh, joyful tears.

They camped that night in peace
    where all the rivers ran
all wanderings were over
    a new world now began
their journey was beginning
    to serve this Son of Man.

GOLDEN DINGO

You, tireless Lover of humanity
    are like a great golden dingo
often misunderstood and misjudged
    falsely accused and hunted
ever the hope of the meek
    and the food of the hungry.

You pad on relentlessly
    through the darkest of nights
seeking the best foods
    for your little ones
who rarely comprehend
    the risks you take for them.

Yet when you come among us
    at morning, noon, or midnight
with the warmth of your presence
    offering the most costly of meals
and we see your bleeding wounds
    we are lost in utter Awe.

BODY AND BLOOD

It is, yet is not;
this is the wonder
of bread and wine
the utterly Divine
now Body and Blood.

Nothing has altered
yet all has changed;
Presence most real
in this one meal
of Body and Blood.

Larger than space
transcending time;
now in our veins
sweeping our brains
his Body and Blood.

Here the prime grace
and the ultimate
mystery has begun;
we are now one
with Body and Blood.

All thanks to this Man
all thanks to this God:
Wonder and praise
all of our days
for Body and Blood.

BUSH BALLARD JESUS

John 6:1-13; 59-61; 66-68

He was just a country bloke
and you knew it when he spoke
but he came with Light-full words
unlike any heard before;
He taught those who would listen
and his kindly eyes would glisten
as he laid his hands on lepers
and gave good news to the poor.

The mobs soon gathered thickly
with their lonely and their prickly
for he always had time
for those of 'lesser breed;'
There were many folk who saw him
and a few good souls were for him
yet many came just for a laugh
or for a 'freebie' feed.

But when he spoke of losses
and of carrying their crosses
enthusiasm wilted
and they turned for home again.
It was not unexpected
that he soon would be rejected
for egos are not keen
to share another's pain.

He turned to his disciples
fearing they had scant scruples
and he put it to them sadly:
"Will you also go away?"
Though some hangers-on absconded
it was Rocky who responded,
"You offer life that's boundless,
and we are here to stay."

He smiled then, almost shyly
knowing Peter was not wily
and seeing love crush fears
that flicked across each eye.
That night he spent awake
praying until daybreak
for he was just a young man
who did not want to die.

MARY OF MAGDALA

Some say Mary was possessed
by demons that made her their nest;
but when Jesus came by
he heard her crazed cry
and made her a woman much blest.

Some claim she was just a tart
who worked the Magdala mart;
but Jesus knew better
than judge by law's letter
and led her to worlds apart.

Some reckon they had a love-pact
"a relationship" to be less exact;
the story sounds good
to babes in the wood
but theories don't constitute fact.

Why are people fascinated so
with a woman who lived long ago?
'Praps she makes Christ seem more real
in an age where the deal
is to keep God out of the show?

LEPERS, JESUS, AND US

Mark 1:40-45

Just another leper
the better left unseen:
"Truly it is their own fault
for not keeping clean."

Just another Aids case
now hidden well away:
"They've brought it on themselves
promiscuous or gay."

Just another boat person
left in detention to stew:
"They've only got themselves to blame
by trying to jump the queue."

Just another drug addict
shooting up behind a shed:
"Don't waste your pity on such trash
they're better off dead."

Just one determined Jesus,
with hands most blest:
"Come to me, all you burdened folk
and I will give you rest."

LUNCH HOUR CHRIST

I see him busking in the mall
where people hustle by;
his oboe plays a haunting tune
that keeps my woes at bay.
    I watch his eyes upon the crowd
    that mass of many moods,
    he seems to play for one and all
as if they each were gods.

His tune keens down to secret depths
then soars above the stars;
but few keep listening for long
their minds fixed on their cares.
    I watch him busking in the mall
    his oboe tunes my soul;
There are a few coins in his cap
but grace is not for sale.

I leave him busking in the mall
as now its starts to rain;
the shoppers run for dry arcades
while he plays on alone.
    He's waiting back at home for me
    when I enter from the street;
    He asks me how my day turned out
so I kneel at his feet.

DEEP WATERS

When heaven's windows seem closed to me
and prayers seem futility
don't come at me with attitude
or cower me with platitude
but let me share the waters awhile
with my Mate from Galilee.

When the church seems to leave me dry
and no God seems to heed my cry
don't look askance and say to me
you'll condescend to pray for me
but let me share the waters awhile
with my Mate from Galilee.

When the Dove of peace seems far away
and words seem dust in the creeds we say
don't think me lost in vanity
or that I speak profanity
but let me share the waters awhile
with my Mate from Galilee.

SO MUCH FUN

Mark 12:29

They met one Guy who loved his God
and made it seem such fun;
he always has a smile to share
and time for everyone.

He told them tales that made them stop
and, puzzled, stroke their chin;
sometimes he used a scalpel word
that got under their skin.

He'd place his hand upon a neck
when it was all uptight;
his touch would drain dis-ease away
and make the load seem light.

He neither boasted nor condemned
and never was one-eyed;
he simply did the best he could
God was his only pride.

He would not try to force his will
on those who heard him preach;
he wanted each of us to know
the God within our reach.

He ended up upon a Cross
where his foes made him pay;
but it seems that He's still around
and never goes away.

THE KISS OF LIFE

John 20:22-23

Come through our locked doors,
persistent lover;
come where we're in hiding
and blow our cover.

Come through our disbelief
enter and meet us;
with your disruptive peace
come in and greet us.

Come past the anxieties
when old fears molest;
fill us with your own breath
that we may know rest.

Come with your saving grace
to lives sore and stale;
breathe forth Holy Spirit
that we may be hale.

Come with forgiveness
like no one has dared;
breathe in us grace-fullness
that it may be shared.

Come in the evening
with your kiss of peace;
breathe upon your people
that nightmares may cease.

LEGION

Luke 8:26-33

He was the caring type of man
who felt the pain of others
but when this burden got too much
scant help came from his brothers.

They never tried to hear him out
but jumped to quick conclusions
they gave lectures he did not need
and multiplied confusions.

They bullied him and chained him down
and ignored his opinions
they treated him like cheapest meat
of Satan and his minions.

Those many voices drove him mad
their hearts now turned to stone
strong with grief he broke the chains
and went to live alone.

The cemetery became his home
stone slabs became his nest
his troublers stayed away at last
and thought it "for the best."

He made his bed among the tombs
and now slept very well
he did not fear the quiet dead
the living were his hell.

A Stranger sailed across the lake
who did not play their game
he simply sat beside this guy
and asked, "What is your name?"

RICH MAN, POOR MAN

Luke 16:19-31

He did not harm
by word or sword
the beggar at the gate;
just passed him by
without glare or care
and left him to blind fate.

It's a damning thing
to ignore the poor
while gorging yet again;
the gulf is wide
between need and greed
and dogs are kinder than men.

A WOMAN TELLS

Mark 5:25-34

Unclean
I cringed, twelve long years;
    forbidden touch
    and husband's bed;
banned by Holy Writ
    until this Jesus
    came to town.

Defying
male prejudice
    I joined the crowd
    that packed around;
drawn near to him
    by burgeoning
    hope and faith.

Bucking creed
and the old gods
    I forced my way
    among the throng
to touch his alb's hem
    and immediately
    knew I was healed!

He knew it too;
trembling I came and knelt;
    He stroked my hair
    and gave me peace!
No more unclean
    and now I knew
    unclean I never was!

ANOTHER?

Matthew11:2-6

If
there is elsewhere
good news surpassing the joy of Jesus
lead me to it
that I may laugh all day and never sigh.

If
there does exist
a better seer who gives clearer sight and hearing
to mere mortals
may he visit my town and hear my cry.

If
there can be found
a lord with superior healing touch
to this Jesus
may his practice grow and multiply.

If
you should meet one
who makes the halt and lame to fly
then bring him near
that I might rise and soar sky high.

If
there's a lover
who does greater than raise the dead
then bury me
beside the road where this marvel walks by.

If?
I search and see
and hear those many voices
which shout at me
but there is none more like True-God than he!

THE BLIND SEE

Mark 8:24

They brought a village man
who had been long since blind
to Jesus that healing prophet
who got inside one's mind.

Jesus used his own saliva
like a mother's soothing kiss
to anoint those clouded eyes
where something was amiss.

The man exclaimed with wonder,
"I see a walking tree."
Jesus touched those eyes again
and the blind did fully see.

He went back to his village
the gossips all a-chatter,
Bethsaida was now famous
the Healer did not matter.

BY THE WELL

John 4:1-42

The thirsty Jew sat by the well
where once old Jacob used to dwell
but today he came on his own.
    He had no bucket and no rope
    and yet he sat there full of hope
    because he never was alone.

The day was hot, the well was deep
but still the vigil he did keep
waiting to share his drink.
    A lonely woman found him there
    she had a rope yet did not dare
    to speak to a Jewish shrink.

Although he had enough and more
he begged a drink from this deep bore
but she looked askance at him:
    "Do you a Jew ask this of me
    a Samaritan as all can see
    unclean and much a doubter?"

He smiled as one who knew this game
but yet he was not into blame
instead he offered her some water.
    She pouted then and thought him queer
    but this man dealt with grace not fear
    and saw her as God's daughter.

He told her things he should not know
the very truth, no bluff nor show
he recognised her dire distress;
    she found her thirst was being met
    and with her a new course was set
    through faith that came pure gratis.

FOR FEET WASHERS

Mark 10:43-45. John 13:1-10a

Service is not what makes us Christ's,
it's the fruit of belonging.
Humility's not onerous stuff
it flows from quiet believing.

Christ sets us free from claiming rights
it's grace that does the saving.
It's not a chore to share his love
our joys are filled when serving.

They eat his bread and drink his cup
who submit to his dowsing.
Whose feet are washed by Heaven's Child
shall also share his dancing.

MY GOOD SAMARITAN

Luke 10:25-37

As I was coming home through life
some muggers hit me hard;
they stripped me of the things most dear
and left me by the road.

A State MP came down that way
saw me in such dire need:
'The times are tough,' he lamely said
'our budget can't provide.'

A news crew found me bloodied
the camera zoomed in near;
the director said, 'That's great TV'
and left me lying there.

A Stranger came down to that place
and bandaged up my wounds;
He gave me oil and served me wine
and placed me in good hands.

Those muggers seized Him down the road
and bashed Him mercilessly;
they crowned Him with wreath of thorns
then hanged Him on a tree.

IN KAKADU, JESUS WEPT

I found him sobbing
Jesus, the one called Christ
sitting on stone ledge
in the large empty space
under a sloping rock overhang
at Burrungguy.

He did not heed me
Jesus, the one called Christ
but kept staring at painted walls
fingering grinding holes
brooding over the vacancy
at Burrungguy.

He knew as a brother
Jesus, the one called Christ
the inner meaning of this place
where once camp fires glowed
for thousands of years
at Burrungguy.

Never again, he knew
Jesus, the one called Christ
the fires and soft chatter
food, love, and laughter
nor the songs of Namarrkurn
at Burrungguy.

I left him weeping
Jesus, the one called Christ
unable to watch with him
beyond a while in such grief
or with such fierce love
at Burrungguy.

Limerick:
FOR A WIDOW

Mark 12:41-44

There was a woman of Zion
with nought but her faith to rely on
as she came to God's house
wealthy fools saw a mouse
but to Jesus she was a lion.

FOOTPRINTS IN THE SAND

John 6:46-71

The sun shone bright, the crowds were there
the kingdom seemed quite near
but Jesus did not preach to please
so some began to sneer.

He spoke of life that comes through death
his blood and flesh abused;
He asked them all to eat their fill
but they were not amused.

'We cannot stomach this' they said
'he's mad or just a liar.'
In clots of discontent they left
to find some new messiah.

A cold wind blew across the lake
to the remnant on the shore;
'Will you also go away?' he asked
'The tide has turned for sure.'

Quick, as usual, Peter spoke
the first thing in his head:
'Where else can we go dear Lord,
without you we are dead?

From that day on the way was hard
and Judas became sour
'till Christ would all forsaken be
in that his finest hour.

I find myself on that same shore
where crowds saw him in flesh
their footprints are long swept away
but I see his, still fresh!

THOSE WHO WALK WITH CHRIST

Those who walk with Christ
shan't live like lords or kings
but they shall know the hidden Joy
which pulses through all things.

Those who embrace Christ's word
need never fear dismay
though earth and sky dissolve
he'll never go away.

Those who dine with him
will never be mislead
the wisdom of all worlds
hides in each crumb of bread.

Those who die with him
need never die in fear
he says when evening comes
'Now, you be of good cheer.'

HE SET HIS FACE

Luke 9:51

Through haze and dust
there goes the Christ
    with one thing on his mind;
his face is set
hard as cold flint
    going to meet his end.

The anxious twelve
have found no salve
    to soothe their rampant fear;
when one's doubts scoff
the road is rough
    and nightfall is not far.

On Zion's heights
the city waits
    to take on Nazareth's son;
Barabbas snarls
Caiaphas smiles
    with guile as old as sin.

A GRAIN IS BURIED

John 12:24

Let this be admitted plainly:
We shrink from being buried
alive in Christ's mission.
>   Where is hope to be found
>   in grain buried underground?

Why was this fellow Jesus
so uncompromising, blunt
leaving no other choice
>   while the world seems full
>   of options not so dull?

We prefer to seize life
and enjoy its favours
savouring its pleasures
>   without worrying much
>   about the results of such.

Why couldn't he
have made the whole thing
a bit easier for once?
>   "Please yourself," why not say
>   and p'raps "Have a good day?"

Where is the glory
in the precious grain buried
in the dark, chill soil?
>   Why is the easy way sheer loss
>   compared to his bleak cross?

Let this be said baldly:
It defies common sense
this way that Jesus takes;
    yet when we go one mile
    with him, we start to smile.

Limerick:
NICODEMUS

John 3:1-12

Nick came to Jesus by night
hoping to find some new light;
though new birth sounded cool
it implied ridicule
and Nick was much too polite.

THE DONKEY

Luke 19:28-48

This donkey did not know;
yet did he dimly comprehend
who the rider was
who nudged him down the road
among the shouting mob
waving palm branches
through the city gates
with praise that was too brief?

This donkey did not know;
yet did he dimly comprehend
those gentle hands
that guided him on a journey
which pilgrims would recall
for thousands of years
with gratitude and praise
mixed with adoring grief?

This donkey did not know;
yet did he dimly comprehend
that angels and archangels
held their breath with awe
as the Source of galaxies
rode on in humble majesty
towards a holy destiny
that beggared all belief?

SUCH PAIN

John 2:13-22

We were in the temple courtyard
that day when this Jesus came
and walked around among the stalls
at first with shoulders squared
like a centurion on inspection;
but the more he observed
the more his shoulders sagged
like one distressed and overwhelmed
    by some gross indecency
    institutionalised and on display
    without apology
    or any hint of dismay.

We watched him move to near a door
and as the common pilgrims looked on
he took some cord and plaited a whip
before squaring his shoulders once more
and storming among the stalls
he up-ended tables and money boxes
while the traders looked on with shock
to see their gold and silver gods
    rattle across the floor
    while his whip whirled around
    as he drove the sheep and cattle
    from that sacred ground.

The chaos seemed complete
at this unexpected feat:
he never left a job done partly
this young man with the whip.
The thing we remember most sharply
were the eyes of that young Christ
not so much glinting with frustration
nor with hostility or fierce rage;
  but wild with enormous pain
  begotten by pure love;
  pain such as we had not at any stage
  seen before and pray never see again!

GOLGOTHA

Luke 23:26-47

Today
I dared to step much closer
to that man on Skull Hill
than ever before.

I elbowed
through the murderous rabble
beyond the high priest's mob
and stood near Mary and John.

The soldiers
leered at me and one said:
"Take a good look mate,
it might be you tomorrow."

Determined
I went and stood about five
paces from that central cross
and looked up.

Hideous scene;
smell of blood, sweat, and urine.
I wanted to throw up;
the soldiers chuckled.

Then I braced myself
and took a long searching look
at the crucified son of Mary
in his agony.

O his dying eyes!
They turned this way and that
wildly searching for Someone
who was already there.

GARDENER?

John 20:15

If you are just the gardener
    then let me lay to rest
    this whole Christian affair.
If you are just the gardener
    then let me weep alone
    by this slough of despair.

If you are just the gardener
    then let me toll the passing
    of a hope most sublime.
If you are just the gardener,
    then let me go on weeping
    until the end of time.

GOOD FRIDAY

On this day all hell broke loose
the wheeler-dealers had their way
and ravening wolves sprang on the Good Shepherd.

On this day darkness reigned supreme
the Bridegroom betrayed and guests scattered
priests schemed their worst, and Pilate washed his
    hands.

On this day foul Satan grinned with glee
the Good Samaritan was dragged through the city of
    God
and the most merciful of all obtained scant mercy.

On this day the merry old sun hid its face
the pure of heart were crushed as hubris jeered
and hope and faith were buried under the detritus of
    despair.

On this day the heaven's angels were dismayed
mother earth shuddered, lilies of the field withered
the sparrows of Jerusalem fell silent as our Lord felt
    forsaken.

Yet on this very day Love triumphs!
The poor and meek inherit an earth redeemed!
And the pure in heart begin to see the God of their
    salvation!

LAMB OF GOD

The Word as the Lamb
   God as a mere child
the wounded Healer
   left out in the cold.

Where else is such power
   so gently applied
or so much glory
   so humbly displayed?

Despised and rejected
   acquainted with grief
man of our sorrows
   bridging the gulf.

The loving beauty
   without shade or sham;
the wisdom of God
   bearing our shame.

Wounded and bruised
   by the tough-willed;
denied and forsaken
   yet saving the world.

Vulnerable then
   up there on Skull Hill;
Love without limit
   vulnerable still.

EMPATHY?

Hebrews 2:14-16, 5:7-10

It was not an angel
but our own flesh and blood
who offered up prayers
with cries and tears
in this school of suffering;
sorely tested like us.

Who need visit Skull Hill
except homo sapiens?
What else truly knows
the crown of thorns
or shudders and groans
at the hammer blows?

We know that awe-full cry
of forsakenness!
While angels praise
the Holy Name
earthlings alone
can share God's pain.

GOD SO LOVED

Mark 15:21-39

So they took him, and he went out
bearing his cross
with the ballast of shame and doubt
which we transferred
upon his shoulders.

They climbed up to a killing place
known as Skull Hill;
a windswept site devoid of grace
until he came
among its boulders.

Up there they then crucified him
between two thieves.
Stray dogs howled as the sun grew dim
as donkeys brayed
and fought their holders.

His jeering foes stood all around
and blood and urine
soaked and stained that desolate ground
as John led Mary away
his arm around her shoulders.

At last it finished for the Son
who writhed no more.
Nothing more could ever be done
leaving us in bleak despair
among the few beholders.

FORSAKEN

No lower pit
no higher peak:
than this man
forsaken.

No crueller grief
no fuller faith:
than this man
forsaken.

No dirtier deed
no costlier gift:
than this man
forsaken.

No darker day
no brighter dark:
than this man
forsaken.

No deeper doubt
no surer truth:
than this man
forsaken.

No sharper pain
no purer peace:
than this man
forsaken.

No larger loss
no greater gain:
than this man
forsaken.

No bloodier deed
no lovelier love:
than this man
forsaken.

No lonelier soul
no nearer God:
than this Christ
forsaken.

BLUE MURDER

A murderer walked free
that day
blinking his eyes at the
bright sky.

A foul murder was done
that day
and all the streams of light
ran dry.

THE THAW

In truth, that unseasonable freeze
that sent us
shivering and huddled behind
closed doors
in rank fear,
lasted only a couple of days
but it felt like the longest on record
and the most
severe.

After the sardonic dawdling
of that time
with our very souls frosted
in a trough
of despair,
new life came leaping and laughing
with blossom on scrub and thorn
and birdsong
everywhere.

This thaw was tumultuous with love
in the air;
as if the last trumpet had sounded
bones rose up
free of grief
to revel with the Lord of life
standing there
beyond belief!

EMMAUS WALK

We trudge along the western road
our heads down hung,
short journeys seem an endless drag
when there's no song.

A stranger joins us in the dusk
humming a tune,
he opens up our grieving minds
to things unseen.

We stop to eat a common meal
at a small inn,
a servant brings a loaf of bread
and cheap red wine.

The stranger slowly lifts the cup
like some rich prize;
breaking the wholemeal loaf
he gives God praise.

That action opens up great rifts
in time and space
we see our risen Friend
and know his peace.

Returning up the darkened road
we run and sing
weary legs revitalised
with this new Thing.

EASTER: IN HIS STEPS

He always did tread this earth with gentle feet
and left tracks in which seeds germinated;
but now, freighted with immortal weight
his gentle footsteps go deeper
and in their fertile hollows
new joys take root.

While on the dusty road to Emmaus Town
where two disciples plodded languid;
he opened Scripture's meaning
and left behind such prints
that even in the twilight
new plants did grow.

At dawn, by a lonely shore of Lake Galilee
he lit driftwood for a breakfast fire;
his feet marked that meeting place
with each loving step he took,
and in each footmark grew
rare seedlings of grace.

With an enemy beside Damascus Highway
where hitherto only thorns had grown;
he etched the scene with footprints
which propagated fruitful vines
so strong that even Rome
grew most jealous.

In latter days to one raw, shy, bank clerk
of a provincial city on the Tamar River;
he came to call and left a spoor
where grew unlikely fruits
such as only Saving Grace
can give account.

Limerick:
FOR A RICH MAN

Luke 18:18-23

He was a clean, wealthy, young bod
who paid due respect to his God
but hooked on his lifestyle
his piety was futile
and he became a sad Mr Plod.

KING IS YOUR WORD

Luke 23:1-5

King is your word not mine;
Friend I am and not very choosey
pagans and prostitutes
taxmen and sinners
grace is my kingdom.

King is your word, not mine;
servant I am, no one beneath me
feet washer and waiter
serving the least
faith is my kingdom.

King is your word, not mine;
physician I am, all free of charge
touching the leper
expelling the demons
health is my kingdom.

King is your word, not mine;
seer I am, seeing God's word
in seed and yeast
wildflower and raven
truth is my kingdom.

King is your word, not mine;
tradesman I am, honing my craft
familiar with wood
hammer and nails
love is my kingdom.

GLORY

John 12:23-27

This matchless Jew
really knew
the difference between fame
and Divine glory.

Where we preen our pride
he took his stand;
from mistrial and abuse
he did not hide.

Where we see cruel loss
and darkest shame
he saw God's awe-full hand
even on a cross.

He went on to end his story
without relenting:
Knowing that his hour had come
he became God's glory.

THE WORD IN THE WORLD

EMMAUS

If this planet's collage
of shapes and colours
were our only light
the sole ground of faith
how wretched
we would be.

If we must deduce
from these alone
the first cause
and final goal
how confused
we would be.

If you, Christ Jesus
had not met with us
on our journey
and opened the Scriptures
how bereft
we would be.

BELIEVING IS SEEING

To eyes that are grace-anointed
and wonder-fully opened:
True Light
begins to irradiate indomitably
throughout this enigmatic scene
glistening throughout all
we thought was fallen
in this sorely opaque world
and through that smidgen which stands tall.

Through red dust of the Outback
from mulga and spinifex:
True Light
in scavenging crows and kites
bracken fern, feral donkeys
hope-full youth so debonair
a business mogul
intractable unionist
and a derelict in the city square.

Nothing is superficial
or secondary about this
True Light:
It is inner, basic, ultimate
an infra-elemental radiance
that saturates everything
and every man and beast;
a living transcendence
redeeming the lost and least.

When it is once perceived
and trusted, even fitfully
True-Light
reveals itself most gloriously
as the indefatigable Spirit
of that Man of Liberation
whose blood mixes with dust
and makes a healing salve
for every person and nation.

AN EASTER DAWN

Back light transforms
the clouds in the east
the swamp hens wake
to greet the feast
at this new dawning.

Against the sky
sacred ibis wend
like angel forms
and there's an end
to hopeless mourning.

The sun comes up
and magpies sing;
Christ is alive
in everything
this Easter morning.

MOMENTS OF WONDER-AWE

The actual cause of wonder-awe
    does not need to be grand:
maybe a lone kangaroo
outlined above dunes at sunset;
a few seconds of a melody
from Vivaldi or Haydn;
a bare wintering tree
lifting arms to the moonlight;
    a phrase from a psalm
    not heard for some time.

Little glimpses of God's realm
    can be gleaned in a moment
unexpected as Christ
unearned as grace;
bud-bursts of wonder-awe
tingling in one's being
    enthralled with the Mystery
    predating the stars!

THIS SINGING JOY

Music: Tallis' Cannon: 8.8.8.8.

There is this awesome Singing Joy
behind all scenes, below, above;
beyond all things yet deep within
one Harmony of seamless love.

By this one Joy we each draw breath
without its Song nothing would be;
no star or planet, lamb or child
nothing at all of land or sea.

Some call it God, Allah* or Yhie*
Bunjil,* Krishna* or Adonai;*
but we have heard its greatest chords
when the young Christ went out to die.

Bread and body, wine and blood
not the cheap tunes of wealth or power;
a Harmony no mortal choir
could shape or hold for one brief hour.

Praise to this Christ incarnate still
praise to this Joy washing our feet;
praise to this Song renewing life
until the Harmony's complete.

*Yhie—an aboriginal 'Goddess' of light.
*Bunjil—sky 'God' of the Melbourne region.
*Allah—Islamic for 'God'
*Krishna—a Hindu 'High God.'
*Adonai—Hebrew for 'Lord"

TO THE LIGHT

To God the light of all that shines
from moonlit lake to galaxy;
in lovers' eyes and a saint's smile:
all praise and glory be.

To God the life of all that breathes
from street to scrub mallee;
emu, lizard, truckie, farmer:
all praise and glory be.

To God the joy of all that sings
from kinder to deep sea;
whales, children, trumpet, flute, and choir:
all praise and glory be.

To God the hope of all who love
from here to Calvary;
self-giving mums and suffering Christ:
all praise and glory be.

PROVIDENCE

Creative Providence:
field lily and raven
wombat and quandong
lorikeet and platypus
rainbow and billabong
seed and gestation
pensioner and nation.

Indefatigable Providence:
parental caring and sharing
in our laughing or weeping
fearing or daring
never weary nor sleeping
joyful as the sunrise
hopeful as children's eyes.

Crucified Providence:
sweating life blood
embracing rough wood
bruised and bleeding
constantly giving
never conceding
dying yet ever living!

OUTBACK SILENCE

'Silence is golden'
    we have heard it said
    but out here it is red:

Red as serrated mountains
    like dreamtime dinosaurs
    slumbering in the sun;

Red as the warm sand
    among the emus-bushes
    and between one's toes;

Red as a desert sunrise
    kissing the ghost gums
    and transfusing the skies;

Red as the blood of the Friend
    who travels with us
    to this world's end.

NEAR ORMISTON GORGE

The sun rises gently, tinting ghost gums,
lazy falcons perch, waiting for an up-draught
as a dingo pads towards her lair.
Our eyes drink in the new dawn
and our souls uplift in invocation.

We light and tend the camp fire
boil a billy, brew some tea
and toast bread on a forked stick.
Our senses respond with pleasure
and our souls ascend in affirmation.

The steepling sun melts the frost
spinifex pigeons arrive for breakfast–
eager like kindy kids at 'play lunch.'
Our hearts delight in their company
and the soul soars high in acclamation.

Water bottles are filled to capacity
a hiker's lunch is prepared and packed;
we stride out into this wilderness
with our whole being vibrant
each step a hymn of jubilation.

WILDERNESS ANGELS?

Cynics see only the hostile
in these wilderness places;
a place for the Enemy
and his angels of chaos.

Sentimentalists ignore
the ugly realities of
life's struggle out here
and the nearness of death.

That realist, the son of Mary
who defied all deceits
wrestled the demons here
and was met by angels of Light.

INLAND JOURNEYS

God of pilgrims
    on those spirit journeys
where our faith
    seems dry as a saltpan
and our prayers
    a cloud of bulldust,
please open within us
    the gift of remembrance.

Stir our minds
    to recall previous visits:
those fresh springs
    we found in barren places;
the wild peaches
    enjoyed in a deep gorge;
that shade sought
    under a rock overhang;
a honeyed shrub
    thriving in desert sands;

And the delight
    that filled us
from a damper shared
    and a cup passed around
with that stranger
    who joined us on track.

WARM WIND

Warm Wind of heaven
    moving the face of waters
    twirling tree blossoms
    fostering bush creatures:
visit our untamed places.

Warm Wind of heaven
    activating human clay
    raising consciousness
    stirring immortal longings:
fill up our empty spaces.

Warm Wind of heaven
    calling through leaders
    singing through psalmists
    reforming through prophets:
unite our warring races.

Warm Wind of heaven
    the gift of loving
    the love of giving
    the joy of forgiving:
bless our upturned faces.

Warm Wind of heaven
    overflowing Christ Jesus
    enfolding all the lost
    keeping the church honest:
swamp us with your graces.

SPRINGTIME

Lover of cherry blossom
and buzzing bees
of blue hyacinths
and nesting swallows:
we praise you for changing seasons.

Lover of fresh-green paddocks
and playful lambs
of wild lilacs in bushland
and of cooing doves:
we praise you for joys of springtime.

Lover of golden wattles
and boxing kangaroos
of audacious magpies
and flowing gum trees:
we praise you for energy unleashed.

Lover of slate-smooth lakes
and fluffy cygnets
of sudden thunder storms
and wild daisy fields:
we praise you for the renewal of life.

Lover of tiny bobbing ducklings
and of chuckling children
of sun showers with rainbows
and rosette clouds at dawn:
we praise you for dying and rising.

For all there is an opportune time
a season for all living things:
O bless the Giver, my adoring soul
and with all that is within me
bless and praise God's Holy Name!

PRUNING

Grape growing is not for wimps
    it requires tough Grace;
a caring willingness to wound
    and amputate limbs of the vine
in order to stimulate and shape it
    towards the better fruit and wine.

Grace reads a season's potential
    fights pests, weeds, mildew
supports productive branches
    and severs fruitless fears;
Grace is as free as sun and rain
    and as steely and sharp as shears.

REALITY CHECK

All things plain and functional
all creatures great and small;
all things grim and wonder-full
the Lord God risked them all.

Each poisonous flower that opens
each forest vine that clings
God gave them all a purpose
including all their stings.

Each duty that may bore us
each pebble in our shoes
the grey clouds in the morning
can be for us good news.

All things plain and functional
all creatures great and small;
all things grim and wonder-full
the Lord God risked them all.

The red-backs in the garden
and locusts in the wheat
the fruit bats in the orchard
and summer's prickly heat.

Each mountain we must climb
each tide 'gainst which we swim
each virus there's to conquer
are subjects for our hymn.

All things plain and functional
all creatures great and small;
all things grim and wonder-full
the Lord God risked them all.

The black holes in the cosmos
the fire storms in our sun
the genes that shape our living
God shaped them every one.

God gave us brains to search them
and lips that we might tell
that this life is most awesome
and all things will be well.

All things plain and functional
all creatures great and small;
all things grim and wonder-full
the Lord God risked them all.

THE PSALM OF A HUON PINE

Blessed are you, Providential Spirit
for creating me so quietly and patiently
and nourishing me so generously.
I thank you for the blessed ground
that has supported and nurtured me
from my slender infancy to sturdy maturity.

Thanks for the sunlight that has drawn me upwards
and for the beauty of dusk-light and starlight
that have made long night watches a blessing;
for the gentle mists that often enfold me
and the heavy rains that penetrate to my roots
quenching thirst and replenishing my whole body.

Thanks for my friends and neighbours in this forest:
the gum trees, dogwood, vines, and whipstick
the tree ferns and their smaller cousins
for the celery-top pine on a nearby ridge
that waves to me each new morning
and for the rug of mosses around my feet.

Thanks for the various birds that have visited me,
for those that have made music among my branches
or under my protection have sheltered from storms;
for the pigmy possums that have played along my limbs
and the mother devil that made a lair among my roots
and raised her family of raucous cubs.

I thank you also for the hard and fearsome times
when rough winds tore off some branches
and left me disfigured and bleeding;
and even for that terrible night when a cruel tempest
twisted and ripped out much my upper trunk
reducing me to a desolate and pitiful thing.

I thank you for the miracle of resurrection
for the new life which leapt up from the old;
for the roots that stayed firm and deep
as I learned that your love had not ceased
even though I had wept in my distress
and pitied myself as a forsaken one.

I thank you for my exceedingly long life;
not confined to a brief ephemeral span
as most other living things must bear
but stretching over two thousand summers;
and for those Pascal nights when a full moon
bathes me and this rainforest in beatitude.

Blessed are you, most generous Spirit
for the innumerable days you have given me:
all of which testify that you are indeed
that Holy One who sends sunshine and rain
equally on both the just and the unjust
and does well for all things great and small.

A TESTING PLACE

Always the place of testing
and paradoxically resting:
    the desert knows its own
and nurtures them in ways
that comfortable, urbane folk
    can never find in town.

What city folk see out here–
as landscape harsh and bare
    intolerant of living things
under searing sun and wind–
is to the desert people
    most providentially kind.

Here things mate, seed and grow
such as townsfolk never know
    with roots that dig down far
below the shifting sands
into that sturdy, moist ground
    which wise souls love yet fear.

Here roo and desert oak
spinifex and patient folk
    prophets and Mary's son
will go to any length
trusting Love unseen
    to find angels' food and strength.

CONSIDER THE BIRDS

Luke 12:22-31

Holy Friend
of regal black swan and common sparrow
of gregarious galahs and shy zebra finch
help us to be keenly aware of you.

Holy Friend
of salty seagull and the singing thrush
of wandering albatross and cheeky apostle bird
help us to truly believe in you.

Holy Friend
of raucous wattlebird and gossipping wagtail
of dancing brolga and flocking budgerigar
help us to stake our lives on you.

Holy Friend
of colourful king parrot and cute fairy penguin
of wary cassowary and calling currawong
help us to be enamoured by you.

Holy Friend
of warbling magpie and strutting mudlark
of stalking heron and chirping noisy miner
help us to be judged by you.

Holy Friend
of laughing kookaburra and chirping cockatiel
of skimming pelican and circling kite
help us to put our trust in you.

Holy Friend
of mimicking lyrebird and tinkling bellbird
of cautious jabiru and cheerful Jacky winter
help us to be healed by you.

Holy Friend
of waddling wood duck and bold drongo
of busy spoonbill and diving grebe
help us be empowered by you.

Holy Friend
of chattering lorikeet and mimicking parrot
of plumed egret and diving sea eagle
help us be enthralled by you.

Holy Friend
of shy reed warbler and tiny sunbird
of pacific gull and peaceful dove
help us to be at one with you.

SEVEN A.M.

A light frost
dusts the shaded slope;
the rising sun
fondles the valley;
a flock of wood ducks
spatter the smooth lake;
a flight of swallows
trawls the air for insects;

and my soul
trawls the morning
for some glimpse
of that First Glory
which precedes
the birth of suns
yet empties itself
among us,
full of saving grace
and loving truth.

WARRUMBUNGLES

Yesterday
I rose early
to see emu and 'roo
feeding among grasses
deep-iced with frost;

Their familiar forms
framed against bushland
folding and steep-sloping
up to the Breadknife
and Belougery Spire;

Already this memory
is fixed and stored
and is now an icon
which I may visit
in later plodding times–

on grey days when I feel stale
and world-weary
among myopic goals
petulant, trite prayers
and inconsiderate deeds.

ONE SUNDAY AT SEASIDE

It has been a good day
shared with my dearest friend:
worship and the Word let loose
a chat with fellow followers of the Way
a climb among the green hills
a swim in bouncing seas
the flavour of newly baked bread
an engaging book to savour.

But it is in the deep dusk
that the best of all arrives:
a chorus of kookaburras
open up a rift in my awareness
and in a rush of pure joy
I sense intimate Eternity
and that Grace that holds
and heals my fragile being.

BUNYA MOUNTAIN'S HOLY SPIRIT

With eagles, Spirit soars above the pines
with pademelons she nibbles young grass
with brush turkeys she hunts for berries
    among these mountains.

In vine thickets Spirit shelters pigeons
in flowing creeks she composes songs
in misty rain she nurtures mosses
    among these mountains.

Children skip through her green cathedrals
old folks glimpse Spirit at their picnics
each gorge and peak declare her glory
    among these mountains.

THE BIRDS OF THE AIR

I commence each day
watching the many birds
which in my neighbourhood
visit, feed, and play:

Minors, magpies, mudlarks
rosellas and red-rumped parrots
galahs, corellas, cockatoos
wood and black ducks;

Wattlebirds and ravens
honey eaters, welcome swallows
royal spoonbills
sacred ibis and sparrows;

And on special mornings
honoured by the visits
of pelicans, swans
and elegant great egrets;

They go about their business
as if we land-bound
cumbersome homo sapiens
do not even exist;

Singing and nesting
chasing each other
Like athletes doing laps
circling the lake

With vibrant energy;
feeding on worms and insects
teaching their young to fly
and share the liberty.

O Eagle of Heaven
and Mistress of the Wind:
guide us up also, higher towards
True-Light of True-Light!

LET THERE BE LIGHT

God of sunlit coolabahs
God of camp fires in the night
God of rainbows and the stars:
Let there be light.

God of holidays and fun
God of laughing girl and boy
God of waves and sparkling sun:
Let there be joy.

God of friends from youth to age
God of the peaceful dove
God with us at every stage:
Let there be love.

You bear our sins and fears
you wipe away our tears
you die for our release:
Grant us your peace.

Then when we laugh, or cry
then while we sing, or sigh
then as we're born, or die:
Grant us light, now!
Grant us joy, now!
Grant us love, now!

MANY ROADS?

Those who appear
shy of arriving
    claim there are many roads
    to take and explore
if we would find at the last
relax by and delight in
    the awesome face
    of the Eternal Ocean.

But aren't they weary
of the roads
    that promise to lead
    to spectacular promontories
or golden beaches
yet which peter out
    among rocks or sand hills
    short of the Eternal Ocean?

An erstwhile colleague
once advised me:
    "It is much better
    to travel hopefully
than to arrive
at journeys end".
    Not from where I am,
    my old friend!

That Limitless Ocean
where I now bathe
    and some days dare
    out of my depth offshore
makes any anticipation
or even special campsites
    on the journey
    seem like a bore!

LIKE MANNA

Entranced
at sweet-sour dusk
we watch the west
where wild geese
fly in restless quest.

Briefly
we savour a joy
which cannot be stored
but like true manna
its Source Adored.

ON THE ROAD:
DISCIPLES TODAY

MY FACE

I met this fellow
with my face
yet wore it with
amazing grace.

I asked him who
he thought he was
what was his game
or what his cause?

He looked at me
with searching eye
and gave me this
succinct reply:

"I am the one
you yet shall be
if you leave all
to die with me."

THE CALL

Called and sent;
though we may prevaricate
argue and gesticulate
the call does not relent.

Called and fed;
though we may try cheaper stuff
or bellyache when things are tough
the call's our daily bread.

Called by name;
though we lag and grow weary
grumble and become dreary
the call still stays the same.

Called by grace;
though we hoist a rebel flag
label the faith a heavy drag
the call remains in place.

GOLGOTHA FAITH

I hack my way
through jungle doubts
hearing the roar
of feral fears.

I climb that hill
where ruins lie
to stand where Christ
shed bitter tears.

Up here among
the stone and thorn
I lift the cup
and toast the dawn!

Limerick:
TO SEERS

Life is not what it at first seems
gold weighs much less than seers' dreams;
men measure and strobe
dissect, test, and probe
yet miss the Awe in the seams

HAPPY THE MEEK

Delight in the rain
after the drought;
joy in believing
after the doubt.

Peace at evening
following the squall;
resting in grace
following a fall.

Wind from the East
filling the sail;
Spirit of truth
when others fail.

The hug of a friend
when I'm forlorn;
the embrace of God
all things reborn.

Love casts out fear
un-cramping the soul;
the pure salve of Christ
making things whole.

Happy the meek
who inherit the land;
Christ and merriment
go hand in hand.

UNFINISHED SERMONS

Great Friend, how can it be
that you, by whom I am called,
confound my sentences
like kites in turbulent air?

A hundred themes or more
that start out full of verve and hope
to tell it as it as it really is
go bankrupt and fall in a heap.

I know I'm not the first
and I shouldn't take it personally;
far bigger minds than mine
have floundered most dismally.

Our wise creeds and dogmas
that seem so fixed and safe
can become just the ravelled sleave
of over-familiar belief.

Even our cherished hymns
become feathers on the wind;
too frail to bear the Weight
that raptures heart and soul and mind.

Let's face it, awesome Friend
I must fall short, missing the best;
my sermons like half-finished homes
whose builders have gone bust.

THE NEEDLE'S EYE

Matthew 19:3-26

It seems a glittering world
on this side of the eye
but it's actually confined
to things that rot and die.

Each has to become slim
to leave this madding race
and slip through the small grill
to reach God's boundless space.

Tourist baggage can't come
dragged on its squeaky wheels
nor leather briefcase fit
stuffed full of shares or deals.

Backpackers find it hard
shop trolleys rarely fit
or brand-name gym bags
carried by sport's elite.

Titles and rank are out
they're much too dignified
and academic hubris
snags like religious pride.

One needs be meek and poor
and naked as a baby
counted as losing life
ranked as a mere nobody.

Only the brave in Christ
escape ego's deadly den
it is excruciating
to become born again.

I'D RATHER BE DEAD

Mark 14:26-31 & 16:56-72

Pete thought he meant what he said
straight off the top of his head
he gave his sworn word
to be true to his Lord
or he would rather be dead.

A servant shamed him instead
with a smirk and a toss of her head,
though Pete shouted and cussed
but she had him well 'sussed'
and Pete now wished he was dead.

ALMOST DISCIPLES?

Mark 8:27-34

Jesus, your teaching seems okay
when taken in small doses
but sometimes you're fanatical
and get right up our noses.

Our life's our own to spend at will
in ways each mood expresses
we're not some mad religious type
that goes to wild excesses

We aim to be most reasonable
not looking for excuses
belief is okay in its place
and the church has its uses.

So no more of this gloomy talk
Jesus, of pain and losses
you cannot really mean that stuff
about us carrying crosses?

THE ROAD NOT TAKEN

Have you ever thought
of the road not taken
the hard choices made
the others forsaken?

Many the junctions
to eastward or west
the high road or low road
which one was the best?

Different companions
different terrain
other openings
with more joy or pain?

Where would I be now
what things would I know
for better or worse
more sunshine or snow?

Would I be wiser
happier and free?
One thing is certain
I would not be me!

WORD OF AUTHORITY

Mark 1:22

Where in the world
can we find one Word
that's there for our benefit
not for the speaker?

We search the newspapers
and visit the libraries
vainly surf the internet
and question gurus.

Emptiness is all we find;
a sophisticated vacuity
or the vanity of fools
self-infatuated.

Is there no conclusion
to the searching and asking?
Is there no answer
to midnight silence?

Only you, great Soul:
Galilean lover of the lost
whose every Word
is soul-valid stuff.

Come then, speak through us;
we've nothing worth saying
but to cherish and echo
your Gospel phrases.

TWO DOUBTERS

John 20:24-29

Thomas and I
were not there that first Sunday
when New Life burst the banks
of the old religion
and flooded reborn minds
with praise and thanks.

Tom was nearby
nursing his grief in solitude
with tearing fierce regrets;
while I was far away
among a people of many gods
who hedge their bets.

So at the first
we missed out on that Peace
which filled their hiding place
and swept away their fears
making them the heralds
of Easter grace.

Thomas and I
were not inclined to trust
on hearsay evidence
a story that we wished could be true
yet seemed to contravene
all common sense.

He, a week later,
was there when the Peace returned
on another Lord's Day
lovingly scattering doubts
like the chaff which the wind
blows far away.

Millennia later
like one born out of season
I stood with the sceptical majority
until that ineffable Peace
humbly came and entered
my poverty.

I have not seen
with these mortal eyes
but I am touched by an 'Amen!'
whose Peace no power on earth
high heaven or deepest hell
can ever stem!

CAUGHT UP

Mark 6:7-13

Not the wise, not power-brokers
neither scholars, nor saints;
    mere ordinary folk
    warts-and-all characters
    like that Peter bloke:
caught up in the freedom of Jesus.

Named, called and empowered
to release the bedevilled:
    the diseased and the lame
    the crazy and the lost
    and the soul filled with shame:
caught up in the loving of Jesus.

Not cluttered with possessions
free as the Wind of heaven;
    inviting the crowd
    anointing the sick
    rebuking the proud:
caught up in the spirit of Jesus.

HOMELESS

Poor restless son
   of a weary motherland
wanders the gutters
and shaken stutters
   craving a brother's hand.

Patronised by his brother
   with a two-dollar conscience
or the supercilious nonsense
of a pair of old boots
   or some moth-wise suits.

Alone this brother
   camps in a park.
Papers restless in the dusk-wind sighing
chorus an infinite, anguished Crying
   which the coming night can't smother.

WOULD-BE SAINT

I thought this soul was truly good
until I heard her claim it;
there's little more disheartening than
the pious who do bray it.

MERCY THAT SURFS

Mercy
that surfs the web
of turbulent time
and says:
'You are saved.
Become what you are'.

Mercy
the alpha mercy
and the omega
wider than time
that says:
'You are mine
I call you by name.'

Mercy
the undiluted joy
at the nucleus
of each moment
saying:
'Come unto me;
I will give you rest.'

Mercy
that sparkling wedding wine
kept until the last
midnight hour:
saying:
'My cup runs over;
drink all of you.'

Mercy
that broken bread
exceeding price
yet shared by beggars
saying:
'I am with you always
to the end of the world.'

ON THE BEACH

John 21:1-9

O Lord of all things made new
how often at daybreak
have you stood on our beaches
but we have not seen you?

You have called out to us
but we have not heard
prepared a breakfast feast
yet we have not cared?

So we go on toiling
from our old leaky boats
or land on barren beaches
to gnaw at stale crusts.

BREAD

I met this man who had no bread
who drew me with the words he said;
He blessed my little and made it more
and handed back the Bread of Awe.

When I had knelt and had my fill
I saw yet more in my hands still:
I shared it with the folk around
and found we were on holy ground.

NO TRICKS

Matthew 12:22-24

The Son of Man has puzzling ways
which some dub 'devil tricks;'
they dig for dirt to throw at him
but nothing ever sticks.

There are no cloaks and mirrors
no guile or slight of hand;
it's Utter-Love that fools those
who will not understand.

BAPTISM

Loving God, we stand awed
in the presence of your evangelist:
this tiny baby thing who dares
to be your child.

Not one word can she speak
this your little messenger
yet in the silence she declares
the living Word!

She has no prior faith
and brings no creed or prayers
but at this font she bears
the faith of Christ!

She offers now no promises
nor deeds of righteousness
but here receives and shares
the righteousness of God!

Helpless she comes today
carried in the arms of others
yet in her helplessness she wears
your massive strength!

Loving God, this is the greatest thing:
Here this child has Brother, Friend,
and Father who utterly cares
world without end!

TO A FECUND GOD

Harrow us with
    furrowed fallows
ready for the season
    of opportunities.

Shape our rough clay
    with deep hollows
and send in dreams
    full of destinies.

Stir the raw mud
    of swamp and wallows
where wait the roots
    of water lilies.

Call back to us
    the welcome swallows
to nest in spring
    under old eaves.

GREAT DIVIDE

There are many smart minds
and many rank fools
who spend their days
among those who camp
on the wrong side of Easter.

There are many good souls
and many corrupt
who become bogged down
among those who camp
on the wrong side of Easter

There are many leaders
and many followers
who live in the dark
among those who camp
on the wrong side of Easter.

There are many god-fearers
and many are godless
who die in the cold
among those who camp
on the wrong side of Easter.

There are a few dear saints
and many of small faith
who have found boundless life
among those who camp
on the right side of Easter.

I HAVE DOUBTS.... BUT

John 20:19-29

I have not seen
I have my doubts
but you have transfused
my life with Life
and I receive.

I have not seen
I have my doubts
but you have infused
my love with Christ's
and I conceive.

I have not seen
I have my doubts
but you have enthused
my soul with Soul
and I believe.

Limerick:
CHRISTMAS PARTIES

Christmas comes but once a year
with partying and forced good cheer
but the more people try
their God-gap to deny
the closer they come to despair.

THE ZOO KEEPER

Mark 7:15

I said to the Keeper at the gate of my mind:
"What brings that shadow across your face?"
He sighed, then replied with eyes sad-kind:
"Any creature that is too proud for grace."

I said to the Keeper at the gate of my soul:
"How many robbers break in at night?"
He answered me in a tone that was droll:
"Less than those who enter by daylight."

I said to the Keeper with the wounded hands:
"Is it hard to keep the beasts inside?"
He replied as one who understands:
"Only when love has withered and died."

Limerick:
POST-MODERN AGE?

Some call this the "post-modern age"
technology is all the rage
but in matters of caring
self-giving and sharing
are we even on the same page?

DIVINE LAUGHTER

We hear your laughter
full of wonder and hope
before the beginning
and of the beginning;
your laughter
overflowing the pre-void void
refulgent with wonder and hope.

We hear your laughter
full of wonder and hope
in the first nano-instant
when all things began;
your laughter
when from nothing all came to be
redoubtable with wonder and hope.

We hear your laughter
full of wonder and hope
when flaming worlds
wheeled into galaxies;
your laughter
when the morning stars sang together
resounding with wonder and hope.

We hear your laughter
full of wonder and hope
as planet earth found its place
with its seas and shores;
your laughter
as prolific life spread around the earth
redolent with wonder and hope.

We hear your laughter
full of wonder and hope
when two persons
first looked into each other's eyes with love;
your laughter
from diverse races, tribes, and cities
resourceful with wonder and hope.

We hear your laughter
full of wonder and hope
when Abram and Sarai
set out in elementary faith;
your laughter
when David sang and Isaiah had dreams
resplendent with wonder and hope.

We hear your laughter
full of wonder and hope
when Mary and Joseph
came to Bethlehem;
your laughter
in common shepherds and angels
relaying wonder and hope.

We hear your laughter
full of wonder and hope
when a Galilean preacher
made friends of sinners;
your laughter
in parables of abundant grace
replete with wonder and hope

155

We hear muted laughter
mingled with awe and grief
when despised and rejected
He stumbled to a cross;
your laughter
with tears defiant over pain and evil
redemptive with wonder and hope.

We hear your laughter
full of wonder and hope
when death lost its sting
and the grave its victory;
your laughter
echoing through the Easter dawn
resurgent with wonder and hope.

We hear your laughter
full of wonder and hope
when Peter found his courage
and Thomas his larger faith;
your laughter
with millions of your common saints
resonant with wonder and hope.

Your laughter
full of wonder and hope
when all things draw together
in universal reconciliation;
your laughter
merry in a new heaven and new earth
reborn with wonder and hope.

THE WIDOW'S MITE

Luke 21:1-4

The rich were in their comfort zone
oozing with self-possession
with tasselled robes and jewelled rings
they made a big impression.

A widow emptied out her purse
the contest most uneven
yet the impact of her small coins
shook the windows of heaven.

SCIENCE

It's wiser to have faith in love
than put sole trust in science
those who only trust their eyes
shall rue such blind reliance.

The ones who can renew the earth
are those with open mind
where science is a form of prayer
there's hope for humankind.

CHOICES

This Lord's Day
is a wonderful day, a terrible bore
a time for laughing, a time for weeping
a day of reconciliation or a day of war.

This Lord's day
is all those things and much more:
whether we are the angry or haughty
or numbered among the meek and the poor.

This Lord's Day
is a time to be brought low or to stand tall
a day for enslavement or of 'rapt liberation
a time to be baffled or a chance to 'get it' all.

This Lord's Day
will never come again to any person on earth;
opportunity hangs on one crux thing:
what gods do we choose to give us worth.

CARETAKER

This caravan park
is watched over faithfully
by a caretaker
with grey hair and green fingers.

She is a single woman
a one-time companion
to wealthy widows
but grown old and discarded.

Home is now a caravan
which she has surrounded
with the gentleness
of ferns and exotic plants.

All the caravan sites
are being transformed
with a variety of trees
and small beds of flowers.

In her aloneness
she has changed a plain acre
into a small sanctuary
of burgeoning beauty.
.

It is a gift to be simple
it is a gift to be free:
may God have mercy
on over-cluttered me.

BREAD IS COSTLY

Winnowing is divisive
there's nothing in between;
the chaff must be expelled
before the grain is clean.

Grinding corn takes effort
skill and power combine;
the mills of love grind slowly
but they grind very fine.

Baking bread's not easy
not some flimsy desire;
the bread that's on your table
has first endured the fire.

The Bread we share is sacred
a paradox divine:
until the Bread is broken
we cannot taste the Wine.

THREE WISE MEN?

Three wise men
proud to be 'post modern guys'
travelled from afar;
One from Sydney
others from Oxford and Harvard
following their secular star.

For each of them
everything on earth is amenable
to scientific reason;
It mattered not
that their trumpeted arrival would be
after the main season.

Flown in ahead of them
were mobile laboratory, cameras
and infra-red eye;
No room for chance
they came with all the technology
that money could buy.

They arrived late,
to let the superstitious pilgrims
get out of the way;
With utmost care
they set things up, while minders
kept the pious at bay.

Proud self belief
moved them around the stable
and to the fabled stall;
Each man entered
sure of what they would discover:
nothing, nothing at all.

After three days
of thorough forensic examination
at that manger scene
three of this world's smartest
claimed there was no Wonder there,
nor had there ever been.

MANGROVES

Maybe they hold a secret
the rest of us should know
the mangroves quietly thrive
where we don't like to go.

They line grey estuaries
and flower in saline sumps;
though they spend life in mud
they're never in the dumps.

PEARLS OF GREAT PRICE

Some like to pray in street and mall
not huddled in a cloister;
this world is not an evil sphere
rather it is God's oyster.

There is a time for sanctuaries
away from crowds that swarm;
there is no crowd to hassle us
when God meets us at dawn.

Remember how young Jacob woke
on a pillow of stone?
"God was in this barren place
where I thought I'd slept alone."

There's ample grit to cause us grief
it's in the best of worlds
and on this oyster-planet earth
that's how God makes his pearls.

THE GRACE OF CHRIST

Romans 3:21-27

There's nothing one can do
there's no way to atone
for when our soul goes broke
we're truly on our own.

The best point we can reach
is when we can't save face
for then we get the option
of turning to free grace.

Christ's grace is always here
in daily nitty gritty;
some are too proud to take it
others prefer self pity.

SALTLESS

Matthew 5:13-16

The absurdity
    of salt-less salt
is only outranked
and out-shamed
by the obscenity
    of faithless faith
and Christless Christians.

RHYMES ABOUT SHEPHERDS

False shepherds smile
their way around
wolves in sheep's clothes
always abound.

Political movers
steal sheep and goats
jumping the fences
wooing our votes.

Stock exchange gurus
backing the odds
laundering their souls
to many gods.

Experts for all things
on TV screen
smoothly dogmatic
proud to be seen.

Voices more voices
filling the air:
"Shepherds for hire
deal if you dare."

One lone Shepherd
killed on a hill
bearing the load
footing the bill.

UNIQUE

No person on this crowded earth
is quite the same
each one is made to be God's child
and outgrow blame
God sees each one as special
and knows each name.

Some say that God can't have the time
for every one
he can't possibly love each geek
under the sun
he's only taken all the pains
with one True Son.

But that True Son did show us all
each is unique
he lived that truth, and all his deeds
this Word did speak
he wasn't God's sole true-love
no divine freak.

I'd rather take Christ's word on it
than cynic's gloom
in God's thoughts and loving heart
there's always room
Love and Peace will cherish us
beyond the tomb.

CONGREGATIONS

They live by faith:
congregations of common people
enlivened by an uncommon gospel
sowing and nurturing mustard seeds.

They live by hope:
congregations growing or dwindling
determined on Christ's optimism
in the midst of the cynical crowd.

They live by love:
congregations with a spirited outlook
looking to serve the world
as they have been truly served.

They live by grace:
defying all the secular odds
in Broome, Bega, and Kings Cross
fellowships convened by God.

SEARCHING FOR GOD?

I met a smart magpie
resting on my back fence
who was on for a chat
of religion and sense:
"I've found farms and towns
parks and city towers
studied sky and landscape
through long daylight hours.
Rainbows and clouds are certainly true
and foxes and eagles are as real as you
but as for the Air that my mother adored
it's not to be found either here or abroad."

I met a smart fish
swimming off Byron Bay
a sharp-witted fellow
with plenty to say:
"I'm on the great search
from here to Fiji
to find that Divinity
that some call the Sea.
I've found great coral reefs, and a volcano's lid
dugong, kelp forests, and a few giant squid
but as for the Sea to which great whales sing
there isn't a sign of that sort of Thing."

ADVENT: WAKE UP

Mark 13:33-37

Wake up! Jump to it!
Be ready for the hour of coming:
where two or three gather
for the breaking of bread
the Master comes quickly.

Wake up! Look alive!
Be ready for the hour of serving:
the stranger and homeless
with the poor and underfed
the Master comes quickly.

Wake up! Get with it!
Be ready for the hour of rejoicing:
at dusk, midnight, or dawn
for the living and the dead
the Master comes quickly.

COMPLAINANTS

We're all in a rush for things rich and plush
but take scant time to sow love;
Yet when later we pick fruits bitter or foul
we whinge against heaven above.

DEPRESSION

Walking down familiar paths
I lose my way
the signposts that once guided me
have gone away
I wonder where I'll rest my head
at end of day.

Change and decay are gnawing at
each weary day
the energy I thought would last
has leaked away
I rarely get the urge to laugh
or seldom play.

The branches where the birds did nest
are bare and dry
if kookaburras start to laugh
I want to cry
when people say they'll pray for me
I'd rather die.

THE GREY FOG

Just when the day
seems brightest
and the weather charts
of my soul
tell me of more
good days to come,

The grey fog arrives
over my horizon
and thickly closes in
irresistibly;
chill and penetrating
to the soul's marrow

Of course I resist;
mock it defiantly
say favourite prayers
recite my creeds
strike at it with my Bible
and scream at it in anger;

But it keeps coming;
insinuating itself
into every crevice
shutting out the sun
and cutting me off from
the warmth of dearest ones

I feel utterly bereft;
unloved and unlovely.
In this grey dominion
only one Voice reaches
with faint flecks of Light
defying my Shadow-land;

There is this one Voice;
one grim foreword
to resurrection:
the One who cries to God
his forsakenness
from an awe-full Cross.

Lord Jesus Christ:
Child of grief and sorrows
Child of Easter merriment:
remember even me
this day as you come
Into your kingdom.

TO ST FRANCIS

A new day has dawned
and before we have yawned
he's up and out with the birds;
each creature and place
is fulsome with grace
as he preaches without any words.

GRACE

Grace
is not a pretty corsage
destined to fade and wither
after a night out on the town.

Grace
is enduring opal
mined from a deep shaft
sunk in a merciless landscape.

Grace
is a costly thing
offered without price
by One who died for it.

A VISION AT FLINDERS STREET STATION

I will always be grateful for the vision–
    that I saw and heard it myself!
I was 'in the Spirit' on a winter's eve
    when three kookaburras came
and sang most gloriously
    outside Flinder's Street Station.

No gum trees being available
    they perched above the clocks,
and as the pallid, July sun set
    along Flinders street
they offered peals of merriment
    to the wintry skies.

The converging commuters
    eager to be on their way home
stopped and gaped at the trio.
    Clients from Young and Jacksons
burst outside deserting Cloe
    and unfinished yarns.

From St. Pauls, worshippers emerged;
    behind them an upstaged priest
standing on the stone steps.
    Trams stood immobile
passengers crowding the streets
    while drivers craned their necks.

Two young police officers
    blew their whistles in vain
before giving up the hassle
    and joining the congregation.
as the kookaburras sang on
    joyfully triumphant!

There were, of course
    as one would expect
clots of disbelievers:
    Some asserted it was a mass illusion
like angels over Mexican cathedrals
    or a Indian rope trick in Mumbai.

Others, of cynical bent, declared
    it was an stunt perpetrated
by Melbourne Uni students;
    just a clever little production
employing holiographs
    and hidden loud speakers.

By grace I envisioned it all;
    hearing the ancient bush vespers
and seeing for myself the surprise
    which transformed into rare joy
on the upturned countenances
    of peak-hour Melbournians.

Under the clocks at Flinder's Street
    has long been a trysting place
    for those meeting a new love.

SORRY BUSINESS?

Where do we go now
God of the poor and the meek
of the lost and those who wait and cry?
Where can be found the wisest song-lines
for our indigenous sisters and brothers
to follow with heads held high?

Saviour Friend
how do we begin to comprehend
those demons with cruel voices
we have set loose among them?
Let alone know how to assist them
to make the better choices?

We do not even glimpse
from afar or see in our dreams
the shape of the promised land
which you have in store for that hour
when we are willing and able
to enter it hand in hand.

Maybe some of our apologies
are starting to flow from repentance
rather than pragmatic guile?
Yet how can we become healing agents
unless we are willing to pay the high cost
and go that second mile?

God of relentless mercy
the truth is that we are frightened;
without them we can't be made whole
yet cannot shape their futures for them.
That really panics us
for we love to be in control.

Maybe we, the "nice respectable folk"
are far more pathetic
and lost in our pretentious speeches
than even their most decrepit remnant–
those who some label 'fringe dwellers'
or 'social welfare leeches'?

Oh indigenous Christ, 'Have mercy
on me a sinner!'
Without your tough, resolute grace
even our better actions
and earnest prayers remain
patronisingly base.

Limerick:
SHE LET HER HAIR DOWN

She let her hair down in his house,
Mr Simon saw her as a louse,
but Jesus saw through her
and gave his peace to her
and sent her home dancing like Straus.

SENT FROM GOD

John 1:6-7

Sent from God: John;
as we too are sent
heralds made of dust
yet with the sacred Breath
inspiring our being
held in sacred trust.

Sent to bear witness
to the unquenchable Light
that shines through darkest dread.
John knew he was a sent man
and for that Light of True Light
faithfully lost his head.

CHRISTMAS CAROL

So happy that morn
when God's Child is born
while proud rulers don't have a clue;
the poor and the meek
like shepherds who seek
see Wonder that makes all things new.

Things snobs label cheap
like peasants and sheep
are granted an insider's view;
while kings and their gold
are left out in that cold
where kindness and love are taboo.

What laughter and bliss
what fun Christmas is
from Mt Zion to old Uluru;
we will sing and rejoice
with all who give voice
with organ or digerridoo.

With poor and the lost
the meek, sad, and least
we share in a wealth beyond creeds;
may God give us grace
as we go from this place
to back up our carols with deeds.

TERRA AUSTRALIS

My Lover has a land, a wide and ancient place
where wildflowers carpet plains, and brolgas dance with
    grace.
You who now share it, your thanks declare it
with guitar, bass and voice:
your praises give
faithfully live
to help this land rejoice.

My Lover has enriched this land with people from of old
who love the soil and creatures, as if they are one fold.
You who now share it, your thanks declare it
with clap sticks, didg, and dance:
your praises give
hopefully live
and give this place a chance.

My Lover mourns dis-ease, brought about by greed
the land itself is aching, waiting for a new breed.
You who now share it, your thanks declare it
by stewardship profound:
your praises give
lovingly live
for this is sacred ground.

HOPE

Our God was in Christ reconciling all things
our God in Mary's Son renewing the world.

The cancelling of debts
and the end of pain and greed
the setting free of broken victims
good news to every child in need.

The wolf shall dwell with the lamb
all war give way to peace
the calf and lion shall feed together and
Arab and Jew embrace.

And the world shall then be rich
with love's liberty
all the lands shall overflow
with the glory of God
as deep waters cover the sea.

Our God is in Christ reconciling all things,
our God is still in Mary's Son renewing the world.

From Kathmandu, Cairns, and Washington
peace will flow like a tide;
from London to Hong Kong
God's arms are warm and open wide
with love for each daughter and son.

Our God is still in Christ reconciling all things;
the healing hands of God in Mary's Son
renewing and embracing the whole world.

SLOW LEARNERS

Mark 9:33-36

One lusted to be the greatest
to make the government his
but when he became PM
he then puzzled:
'Is this all that there is?'

One sang to be the greatest
to make her fans adore
but when she reached her goal
she then fretted:
'Isn't there something more?'

One jockeyed to be the greatest
of bishops in the land;
archbishop by forty five
he then pondered
why joy had turned to sand?

Now they are aged 'has beens'
and living in the past
yet still have not embraced
Christ's relentless word:
'The first shall come in last.'

STONES

Mark 9:42

Many uses,
flintstone, flagstone.

Many joys,
birthstone, gemstone.

Many pains,
gallstone, hailstone.

Many tools,
grindstone, whetstone.

Many tears
gravestone, brimstone.

Many hopes
cornerstone, hearthstone.

One warning
millstone, millstone:

Kyrie eleison
Christe eleison!
Kyrie eleison!

ONE SUNDAY

Outside, it is a dull day
mist and light rain
hanging low over the church
and the birds in trees
not raising a song.

Inside, a motley bunch
of sinners gather
exchange warm greetings,
and prepare to do
a remarkable thing:

They dare make contact
with that First Light
which precedes the universe
and in prodigal grace
once wore a human face.

SCIENCE AND RELIGION

I believe that the world is charged
       with the energy of God
who neither wearies nor sleeps nor ever despairs
but with tenacious love carefully fashions
out of star dust, children of light
and leads them to glory.

I believe there is no conflict
       between science and religion
unless religion becomes self-absorbed and arrogant
or science gets drunk on its own hubris
until it no longer seeks the Light
but its own dismal glory.

I believe we are still living
       in the long, sixth day of creation
where the healing Spirit of God has not ceased working
and never will 'til all is redeemed and consummated
through Messiah Jesus, True-Light of True-Light;
then God will rest in Sabbath glory.

MANY IDOLS

Mark 10:17-22

One idolised wealth, another hungered for fame
so they went sadly away.
One loved career, one the latest fashion
and they went proudly away.

One lived through her children, one lived for his farm
so they went busily away.
One fed on the adulation of fans, sport was another's
    passion
so they went impatiently away.

One had the gambling lust, another's was grog
so they went wildly away.
One wanted to be waited on, one wanted to lie about
so they went sluggishly away.

One was hooked on sex, one on the next drug fix
so they went hurriedly away.
One lived for churchly honours, one for pious clout
so they went blindly away.

MORE: A CREED OF DAMNATION

More bargain sales, more cluttered lives,
more credit cards, more folk on the skids,
more teen models, more bulimic girls,
more club pokies, and more hungry kids.

More sexual tricks, more broken vows,
more porno sites, more sadistic force,
more trial partners, more empty lives,
more mega weddings, and more divorce.

More proud mansions, more security guards,
more deregulation, more laissez faire,
more take overs, more blatant greed,
more global warming, and more despair.

More high-place scandals, more déjà vu,
more glitzy casinos, more dazzled fools,
more law and order, more corrupt police,
more high flyers, and more drug mules.

More speeding cars, more paraplegics,
more bank profits, more repossessed farms,
more exploitation, more suicides,
more gold and jewels, and more burglar alarms.

More on the run, more junk food meals,
more grog to drink, more grief to taste,
more sporting stars, more performance drugs,
more time to play, and more years to waste.

More empty churches, more firework displays,
more self-made men, more exploited friends,
more shopping malls, more crippling debts,
more bad decisions, and more loose ends.

More injustice, more suicide bombers,
more unrepentance, more shifting goals,
more spin doctors, more cynical voters,
more pop cults, and more lost souls.

DO NOT SEPARATE

What God has joined, let no one put asunder,
Creature and Creator, breath and dust;
eternity and time, knowledge and wonder,
love and commitment, risk and trust.

Mind and feelings, body and soul,
church and world, secular and sacred;
faith and deeds, source and goal,
prayer and politics, word and deed.

Travail and birth, growth and decay,
mercy and justice, law and grace;
seedtime and harvest, toil and play,
heaven and earth, time and space.

AGEING AND DEATH

THE LAST HURRAH!

The wear and tear of eighty years
exact their toll;
discarded creeds and false leads
have freed my soul;
there is much less of vain success
yet I'm more whole.

The muscles sag and no more brag
that they can cope;
my joints creak and prove weak
on gentle slope;
I am diminished yet far from finished
I live by hope.

The less I know the more I grow
in metaphor;
it's a delight not to be right
on every score;
the more I lose the more I choose
Christ's gospel store.

When I leave please do not grieve
my empty space;
be glad for me that I am free
of the rat race;
when I am nought I will be brought
home by his grace.

FOUR SCORE YEARS AND MORE

From four score years and more
a few straws have been gleaned;
they're not those easy creeds
from which we're quickly weaned.

God is not any 'Thing'
for things age and decay;
yet there's this timeless Other
who will not go away.

The bound are truly free
the meek stand very tall;
the weak are truly strong
empty folk have it all.

The unseen is true stuff
but solids are a myth;
there is no greater birth
than those pangs we call death.

Through four score years and more
by grace I've learned content:
the Landlord of this scheme
does not charge any rent.

AGE AND DECAY

No more I am appalled and sad
at moth and rust
they go the way that mortal things
all surely must
it is enough to live each hour
in peace and trust.

Age and decay are stripping me
of needless care
at last I know the cost of pride
is far too dear
a little is enough for me
while God is near.

I greet each day with thankful heart
and upturned face
each day is rich beyond my needs
no empty space
my life becomes one song of love
'grace upon grace!'

FLYING WITH THE BIRDS?

In my old age
I still have sweet-sour dreams
in which I join the birds
in riding the winds.

I do not do it very well
there is much huffing and puffing;
I cannot as yet soar high
but by God, I can do it!

In these vivid dreams
I cannot understand
why so few other people
will even attempt it?

ON TRACK

Some days when camped
in barren wastes
where carrion fears
molest and numb;
I find the spoor
of the young Rabbi
and know the best
is yet to come.

KEEPER OF MY SOUL

I will climb upon the Bedrock
    for faith is freehold here;
I will rest upon this Bedrock
    when my load's hard to bear:
friends or those who scorn
    the sweet news and sour
the fears that mock at midnight
    the light that comes at dawn.

I will live upon the Bedrock
    for hope upholds me here;
I'll serve others from this Bedrock
    for giving is true prayer:
kiss of peace or thorn of pain
    my strength, and all my shame
vows nurtured through the tempest
    each step when I am lame.

I will love upon the Bedrock
    for Love enfolds me here;
I'll lie down upon this Bedrock
    trusting as Christ's joint-heir:
sound asleep or restless
    the distant stars above
clutching life, wanting death
    there always is this Love.

I'll grow old upon this Bedrock
    for Grace strong-holds me here;
I will die upon this Bedrock
    and death shall be no more:
with all I have and all I am
    each triumph, every flaw
I come to my Holy Friend
    to love and ere' adore!

NURSERY

Earth is no finishing school
to polish almost-saints;
it is for misfit souls
God's nursery for 'quaints.'

Those who think they are wise
have lost the simple plot;
no one has cause to boast
archangels we are not.

Yet one guy really did make it
though many thought him odd:
that Man from Galilee
who overflowed with God.

AT DAY'S END

At the end of day
my bruises set the mood
the toil seems rarely
worth the scant reward;

I turn to prayer
pondering if all is vain
if dust is dust
and ever shall remain?

But then I soar with
the eagles of Christ's dreams
and know that life
is nobler than it seems.

A PREACHER LOOK BACK

Some fields where once we sowed good seed
have turned to stone;
the reapers who once laughed and sang
are now all gone;
the barns where we then danced with joy
stand all forlorn.

On hills where sheep found ample feed
the wild goats own;
where shepherds once knew each by name
the wolves now roam;
the folds that sheltered from the storm
have tumbled down.

The plots where now the preachers toil
have marginal soil;
yet though the ground is hard to work
they give their all;
and there's rejoicing when there's gleaned
one precious soul.

CLOUD OF WITNESSES

Hebrews 12:1-2

The Lord's Day arrives on golden wings;
and once more I find myself surrounded
by that "great cloud of witnesses"
whose ranks grow ever more glorious.

Once, I visited the ruins of Delphi;
climbed to the amphitheatre
and sprinted one length of the arena
imagining the roar of cheering crowds.

Now it's a weekly, Lord's Day affair
with a numberless congregation:
John and Luke are there with Mary,
Paul, Priscilla, Eunice, and Timothy;

Smiling Monica with her son Augustine,
Francis and Clare, Abelard and Eloise;
Luther is waving, and Susanna Wesley,
Bonhoeffer, Teilhard, and Pope John XXIII;

My grandparents, Alma and Annie with
lay preachers Walter and Robert side by side;
Mum and Dad and my smiling sister Margaret
who preceded them by over fifty years.

Wilfred, at whose side I first confessed the faith;
George, Jess, and Ron– still looking surprised;
Viv, Ray, Betty, Guv, June, Mike, and Rosalie
and recently inducted– Don, Dorothy, and Rod.

The light perpetual transfigures all as I join them,
taking courage to finish my race with 'even joy',
my aged voice blending in the one mighty anthem
from their tiered ranks: "Now thank we all our God."

OLDER AND WISER

From branches of trees once lopped
the bellbirds chime.
Through valleys where I used to rush
I now take time.

Those rambling vines I once did curse
have borne ripe fruits.
Beneath the flowers I thought were new
I find old roots.

In pet theories I thought were wise
appear deep cracks.
On paths where I felt all alone
I find Christ's tracks.

MIRACLES?

What others claim
I don't decry
but miracles
have passed me by:
there's been no cloud
no burning bush
no Naaman's ass
to give a push.

There has been one
defining thing:
a grace-full Source
that makes me sing.
It comes as free
as sun and rain
to bring both joy
and growing pain.

It can't be bought
it can't be sold
it sought me young
and finds me old;
this Source once wore
a human face;
He is my one
redeeming Grace.

PROMISE

Instead of cruel thorn
shall flourish the grape vine
nettles, weeping, and pain be no more;
gum tree and Norfolk pine
shall sing and clap hands
'rap at those joys God has yet in store.

When plains of gibber stone
become rich barley fields
we will all know we don't toil alone;
while others complain
of drought and poor yields
we'll celebrate this new season's grain.

When weeds of every place
give way to spring flowers
we will witness the power of free grace;
while some grow bitter
live for cheap glitter
we'll walk with Christ's light on our face.

When the dark vale of death
is garden of rebirth
we'll know that the darkness can't win;
while others don't care
or slide into despair
we'll be ready and keen to begin.

Instead of the cruel thorn
shall flourish the grape vine
nettles, weeping, and pain be no more;
gum tree and Norfolk pine
shall sing and clap hands
'rap at what our God still has in store.

AGEING BLUES

Old age is the reflection
in glass as you pass by
that stranger wearing wrinkles
who makes you want to cry.

Old age is a caper
where there's no guarantee
mind and flesh are partners
that don't often agree.

Old age is that beggar
that stood outside our gate
it now has taken over
and makes us stand and wait.

PROGNOSIS DIMINISHMENT:
PARKINSON'S PLUS

When first I heard of my cruel demise
I was upbeat;
it seemed to me it gave opportunity
for noble retreat;
I did not know as I know now
how tedious that feat.

Diminishment of limb and mind
my destiny;
inexorable the steady decline
has proved to be;
I'm slow to find and taste the fruits
of its strange liberty.

Yet by the grace of that Gospel Man
I am okay;
The less I'm able to pick and choose
and have my say
the closer am I to his word
and unique way.

Not my will but yours, my God,
now be done;
In diminishment I go the way
my Lord has gone
and share the last shalom of the
Forsaken One.

CHRISTMAS NEAR EIGHTY-SIX

Near eighty-six there are no new tricks
as Christmas comes yet again;
I still remember days of December
when childhood was my domain;
after a short night I woke at first light
to leap on the gifts by my bed;
eating and drinking (my stomach not shrinking!)
the rest of the day quickly sped.

But now I am old I'm no longer sold
on pleasures that come and go
from joy and the tears of the turning years
there's one sure thing I do know:
In comfort or tatters nothing else matters
'cept that Event in the straw;
as I kneel before that I know where I'm at
and shall not want any more.

THE END IS NOT YET

Mark 13 & Romans 8:18-25

When you hear war, and rumours of war
the end is not yet; just wind and tide;
these are birth pangs of mother earth
in travail with children of God.

Don't be mislead, don't grow anxious,
do not follow men of high pride;
keep your hearts true, all will be well,
slow turn the years, patient is God.

When you're abused, if you are beaten
do not lose heart, I'm at your side;
don't practice speeches, nor try slick words,
just tell the truth, honest to God.

I'll show the way, the Spirit your Friend,
just keep the faith, however you're tried;
though friend forsake or child betray
keep wide awake, faithful is God.

Temples shall fall stone upon stone,
rubble and dust, all human pride;
watch through night storms, be there at dawn,
when the end comes, you'll know your God.

HUNGER AND THIRST

There is a restlessness in me
which as yet
neither faith has satisfied
nor love expelled.

I have drunk
from the wells of salvation.
I have eaten
of the manna from heaven.
No other drink
gives any such delight
no other bread
so nourishes my being.

Yet still I am
thirsty and hungry
for more.
Should I diagnose
a serious flaw
in my believing?

Or is this rest-
lessness the joy-anguish
of those blest
with a foretaste
of That which is
deeper than time
and space?

I wait for the
consummate blessing
of those who hunger
and thirst.
I wait
hungry and thirsty
for that which
I already have.

Limerick:
MY NAME IS PAGED

I was that child so very young
I was the song my mother sang;
but now I am aged
I hear my name paged
in a different Mother Tongue.

HOMESICK

Really, home-sick for God?
I must be mad to confess it
others may think I'm odd'
but I'm ready to profess it.

These sweet-sour pangs have gnawed
since my springtime youth;
in teenage years I'd deny it
by playing 'Hide the truth.'

It came on strong in mid-life nights
watching a summer moon
reading a poem or Psalm
or ravished by a Mozart tune.

In these final autumn years
its ache is sometimes vast
and fuels my yearning thirst
to reach God's Home at last.

LIGHTS OUT?

If lights go out "for keeps "at death
you won't hear me complain.
Life is a gift that is sublime
unearned as sun and rain.

But that young guy from Galilee
knew what it's all about
throughout his life so full yet brief
his love was full of clout.

He reckoned there is more to life
than this spot in the sun
that when for us the lights go out
the fun has just begun.

In spite of those grim, driven souls
for whom death is forlorn
I'll bet my all on Easter Day
and Christ's greeting at dawn.

A WORD WITH GOD

You and I
are not strangers.
Before I was conceived
in my mother's womb
you smiled
and whispered my name
and in your love
knew my whole frame.

You and I
are not strangers.
After the undertaker
took me away,
you smiled
and called my name
and without fear
to you I came.

You and I
are not strangers.
In your eternal joy
(while I kneel here)
you smile
and sing my name
and I am alight
with your flame.

CHILDHOOD AND OLD AGE

Wonders were the common stuff
when I was but a child:
Jack and Jill went up the hill
Jesus was meek and mild
Humpy Dumpty sat on a wall
a cow jumped over the moon
Mary had a cuddly lamb
the dish ran away with the spoon.

Wonders do not often happen
now that I am old;
Little is new under the sun
and winter's always cold;
Politics don't create hope
friends grumble and decay;
tomorrow is an uphill climb
and I'm too weary to play.

Yet by some alchemy of grace
there is one Wonder-Light
that neither pain nor storm can quell
not even death's deep night;
it hangs around out in the cold
unless invited in,
then in its glow I find that Warmth
where wonders still begin.

SOME JOYS OF OLD AGE

Old age is a boatman
that rows against the tide
it dares to face the questions
that once we put aside.

Old age is a bonus
for having been so young
past melodies still please
the best yet to be sung.

Old age is a sifting
of things that have long gone
it comes to make its peace
with the things left undone.

Old age is a good friend
not a poor empty husk
she's filled with memories
and sits with us at dusk.

Old age is the freedom
from competitive stress
kudos no longer matters
no need now to impress.

Old age is a challenge
young athletes can't conceive
death brings the final hurdle:
end well and we'll receive.

DEATH

There you are again
old spook
lurking in the shadows
like some cheap soap opera
private eye;

Or rattling old bones
in the night
as you have often done
from our childhood fears
to old age.

Just when we relax
thinking
you might have outgrown
your idiotic stunts
and lame games;

Or 'praps you've been buried
under
the slag heap of our busy toil
or become discouraged
by our faith;

You turn up again
squeezing
through the cracks in creeds
with that silly smirk
on your face;

Pleased as punch to see us
startled
like some cantankerous relative
who delights in turning up
inopportune.

I don't know, old spook
who is
the bigger fool you
or we with our knee-jerk
jitters?

Death, don't put on airs:
Loser!
You're just another con artist
as empty as a garden tomb
at dawn!

THIS TENT

2 Cor.5:1-5

This tent is but a flimsy thing
by night it's damp with dew;
I draw the blanket tightly round
but midnight chills seep through.

This tent is not a lasting home
discomforts breed with years;
I long to rest without distress
relieved of all my cares.

This tent has known too many storms
the fabric's lost its strength;
When winter comes to storm it down
I'll rest well then, at length.

This tent will quickly turn to dust
as I take up another
to pitch my tent by heaven's streams
with my Divine Brother.

THE EASTER THING

Listen, I share
a mystery:
as is was then
so will it be
even for me.

It will happen
in the twinkling
of a new day
when the last stone
will roll away.

Above the sludge
(somewhat dazed)
of ancient fears
and modern doubts
I will be raised.

In that new light
I'll see starkly
and never more
through smoked glass
squint so darkly.

Then I will know
as I am known
my gloomy thoughts
and many deaths
all overthrown.

Eagling I'll rise
without constraint
run on my way
and not weary
walk and not faint.

Sighing will end
on that new day
and sorrow cease
for God will wipe
all tears away.

MY APOCALYPSE

Dread;
the darkest dread
engulfs me
as I recede, recede
into the void.

Rushing sound;
a syphoning wind
sucking me down
relentlessly deeper
into darkness.

Utterly alone,
the hand of my Beloved
clutches for me
but cannot touch
my receding.

Stripped,
of all worldly esteem;
no more husband
father, pastor
wordsmith.

The void
is all that's left
with the rushing
wind of receding
raw dread.

Darkest death.
This is it then
the old Enemy
has won.
The end.

Yet a strange
Knowing arrives
and warms
the scrap that is left
of me.

Somehow
in this darkest-ness
I am free, free
absolutely
set free!

Set free
of foolishness
pomposity
and those questions
that plague.

Stripped of
planning for tomorrow
and regretting things
of yesterday;
now free!

Released
from ambiguities
in this amoral world
and the heavy weight
of integrity.

Somehow
that dreaded
rushing emptying
is utter
kindness.

And now
into this void
No-Thing comes
and smiles
at me:

"Welcome!
You have waited
a long time
for your arrival
back home."

AFTER A BURIAL

When we leave a burial
there seems nowhere to go
no firm step to take
or wise word to speak;

So we usually disperse
awkwardly to begin
silently or with a whisper
singly or in a cluster;

As if expecting something more
some last sign to happen?
We are relieved when it doesn't
yet uneasy that it hasn't.

WITH CHRIST

When the heart is stilled
and the lungs give out
their last sigh of relief
death shall have no sting.

When the flesh returns
to the deep warm arms
of old mother earth
the grave shall have no victory.

When the time has come
for the singing of the birds
and the bushland blooms again
death shall be no more.

SHIFTING CAMP

When I leave this life, Holy Friend,
like a traveller shifting camp
I will trust your Word:
"Eye has not yet seen
nor has ear yet heard
what you have in store."

But of one thing am I sure:
"Trailing clouds of glory
will we come"
from this world
our first, fair home.